MELANCHTHON
SELECTED WRITINGS

MELANCHTHON
SELECTED WRITINGS

translated by
CHARLES LEANDER HILL

edited by
ELMER ELLSWORTH FLACK
and
LOWELL J. SATRE

Augsburg Publishing House
Minneapolis, Minnesota

Rosaliae meae blandissimae dominae
cujus symphonia amoris jam jamque usque
ad hanc ipsam diem manet.

EDITOR'S PREFACE

Doctor Charles Leander Hill passed away suddenly December 8, 1956, leaving unpublished his translations of works of Philip Melanchthon, to which he had given many years of meticulous labor. By the time of his death he had practically completed the translations which he proposed to publish in one volume and had prepared an introduction to the work. As he indicated in his introduction, he planned to carry forward his translations from the Latin, covering Melanchthon's major writings, including a fresh rendering of his *Loci Communes*, the 1521 edition of which he published in its first English dress in 1944.

Recognized through this publication as a real Melanchthon scholar, Doctor Hill received the incentive to continue his translations of the Reformer's works. Early enamored of his "dear Philip," as he, like Luther, often referred to him, he made the study of this Reformer his chief scholarly interest. He had specialized in Melanchthon studies in his graduate work leading to the S.T.M. degree at Hamma Divinity School and the Ph.D. at Ohio State University. With that background, which included also studies at the University of Berlin, he was in position to build a strong foundation for his later researches, to which he gave himself indefatigably even in the midst of administrative responsibilities as president of a university.

Doctor Hill became one of the leading Melanchthon scholars in America. Probably no other scholar has translated into English so many of Melanchthon's writings. What a loss to Reformation research his untimely death has meant!

In view of the widespread observance in 1960 of the four hundredth anniversary of the death of Melanchthon on April 19, 1560, it seems appropriate to publish for the first time in English translation some of Melanchthon's choice works. It is anticipated that many books and articles about Melanchthon will appear during and succeeding this anniversary year. It has been noted that each special Melanchthon anniversary observance—such as the observance of the four hundred and fiftieth anniversary of his birth in 1947—has called forth rich and rewarding Reformation studies which have resulted in fresh appreciation of the man and his work.

In spite of his eccentricities and conciliatory leanings, Melanchthon was truly one of the greatest of the early Reformers. His *Loci Communes* of 1521 was the first compendium of Lutheran doctrine. He was the author of the *Augsburg Confession* of 1530, the mother symbol of Protestantism, the *Apology* thereto, and numerous other important works. Historians and theologians have not fully recognized the rich contribution which he made to the Protestant Reformation. His writings stand as significant evidence of his creative thinking.

Doctor Hill's translations of some of these works from the original Latin will afford English readers a far better understanding and appreciation of Melanchthon than was hitherto possible for them to acquire. For this reason it has seemed incumbent upon the editor, into whose hands the manuscript fell following President Hill's death, to attempt to prepare it for publication posthumously.

The editor undertook the task in the hope that he might have the work completed in time for publication in the Melanchthon quadricentennial year 1960. He found it necessary to rewrite the entire manuscript, altering here and there sentence structure, phraseology, punctuation, paragraphing, and translation. Melanchthon's Latin sentences are generally long and involved. Doctor Hill attempted to provide a literal translation from the Latin, so as to reproduce as nearly as possible the thought structure of the original writer. For the most part, the long sentences have been followed in the English rendering after comparison with the Latin text. To be sure, the reader will find this cumbersome, but it must be borne in mind that the translation is from the Latin of the sixteenth century and not from a modern foreign tongue. The aim in the translation has been to reproduce Melanchthon as realistically as possible.

A ready linguist, Doctor Hill introduced into his manuscript numerous Latin and Greek phrases and sentences. Since few readers would be at home in these languages, the editor has taken the liberty to translate these parts also. Where the English text digresses in meaning from the original Latin let the reader charge the incongruity to the editor rather than to Doctor Hill, whose knowledge of the Latin idiom was superb.

For the benefit of students of Reformation thought the editor has appended a selected bibliography on Melanchthon.

The preparation of these selected materials from Melanchthon, which Doctor Hill so carefully translated, for publication posthumously has truly been a labor of inspiration, appreciation, and affection.

ELMER ELLSWORTH FLACK

Springfield, Ohio, April 19, 1960
In commemoration of the
four hundredth anniversary
of the death of
Philip Melanchthon,
April 19, 1560

TRANSLATOR'S INTRODUCTION

As is well known, particularly in Protestant circles, a Melanchthon Jubilee was held in 1947 in recognition of the four hundred and fiftieth birthday of the *Praeceptor Germaniae*. Various phases of Melanchthon's theological and literary activities were brought anew into contemporary focus. In 1948 a group of theologians in Germany set for themselves the task of publishing a *Studienausgabe* of the most important works of this Reformer.

Professor Dr. Friedrich Karl Schumann was the moving spirit of this new venture. Ten years prior to this time the scientific investigations into the history of the Reformation had accentuated the need for an improved and more useful edition of Melanchthon's works. Previously, the bulky and often inaccessible *Corpus Reformatorum* series, edited by Bretschneider and Bindseil in twenty-eight volumes, had been the chief literary form of Melanchthon's works. In 1897 the *Verein für Reformationsgeschichte* undertook to supply the works which were missing in the *Corpus Reformatorum* by supplying in five volumes the so-called *Supplementa Melanchthoniana*.

In 1926 O. Clemen began to assemble the letters of Melanchthon and completed the first volume containing the correspondence between the years 1510 and 1528. His death precluded further work by him on this project. His first volume, however, pointed up for us for the future an entirely new method of investigation into the works of Melanchthon.

For more than a century there has been felt a great need for a good and useful edition of Melanchthon's works. This need has been supplied by a group of German scholars who have undertaken the publication of a five-volume edition of Melanchthon's works. In 1951-52 appeared the first two volumes of this projected work. According to the plan, Volume I, edited by Robert Stupperich, embraces theological writings; II, 1 and 2, by Hans Engelland, dogmatic works, the *Loci Communes* of 1521 and 1559; III, by Gerhard Ebeling, Melanchthon's major exegetical works; IV, by Richard Nuernberger, philosophical and historical writings; and V, by Hans Volz, correspondence.

In the first two volumes of the series there are released copious notations and references which constitute a distinct improvement over the *Corpus Reformatorum* series. Moreover, the editors have made many changes in the Latin spelling, removing many obsolete and archaic forms and bringing the texts into conformity with classical Latin spelling. While Melanchthon often quoted from both the *Vulgate* and Luther's German Bible, the editors agreed to employ all citations from the latter.

Since the publication in 1925 of the monumental work of Theodor Kolde entitled *Die Loci Communes Philipp Melanchthons in ihrer Urgestalt,* there have appeared several very important works by outstanding scholars dealing with various themes about Melanchthon, indicating that German Lutheran scholarship is more and more coming to regard Melanchthon's contributions to the history of Protestant thought in a more favorable light.[1]

The works of Melanchthon which I have selected for translation are dated between the years 1519 and 1539. They are by no means the only documents of the Reformer which appeared during those years, but I have selected them because they are highly representative of his theological development during this important segment in the history of the Protestant Reformation.

Characteristic of these works is the fact that they are grounded thoroughly in the holy Scriptures and in the best and most trustworthy traditions of the ecumenical or catholic church. Melanchthon's strong opposition to Roman Catholic distortion of the truth of Scripture and the vital principles of the Apostolic Church drove him, in the interest of the new evangelical doctrine, to an absorbing preoccupation with the fathers of the Eastern Church. He seems to hold that the true tradition—insofar as we may attach historical trustworthiness to tradition—in many instances has been preserved

---

[1]The reader is referred to the selected bibliography appearing at the close of this volume.—Editor.

within the Eastern Church. It is well known how fond he was of the Greek Catholic Church. His willingness to discuss matters impartially and objectively with the Eastern theologians and, for all that, with the Roman and Reformed wings of Christianity, has been the chief factor in the charge made against him that he was too irenic and too much interested in church union.

Recent movements within Protestantism and the orthodox church in terms of ecumenicity, however, serve to soften the criticism which historians and dogmaticians have customarily made against Melanchthon on this point. It seems to me that no history of the Ecumenical Movement can be properly written without giving him an exalted position in the stream of its development.

Before each translation I have prefixed brief comments which, I feel, will orient the reader's mind in a general way to what follows and will serve as a means of introducing him critically to the particular works. These comments are based directly on the forewords to the Latin texts which were prepared by the various editors of the *Studienausgabe* referred to earlier in this introduction.

I am greatly indebted to the editor of the *Lutheran Quarterly* for permission to reprint two articles which I had submitted to that journal.[2] With the exception of those two articles, all the materials of this volume represent works of Melanchthon hitherto unpublished in English.

I have followed the same policy here which I adopted as a guiding principle in my translation of the *Loci Communes* of 1521.[3] That is to say, I have made the translations as literal as possible without becoming cumbersome in the English idiom. For all that, I want the voice of Melanchthon to resound in these works in as clear a manner as possible.

The translation of this arbitrary series of works will serve to fill the interim until I can complete the final translation of the *Loci* of 1549, which is the last form of the editions of 1521 and 1535. With the appearance of the last edition of the *Loci* of 1549, interested persons will have an opportunity to make a comparison of the materials and then in the light of such comparison to decide for them-

---

[2]"Melanchthon's Propositions on the Mass," *Lutheran Quarterly,* Vol. VI, February, 1954, pp. 53-57; "Some Theses of Philip Melanchthon," *idem,* August, 1954, pp. 245-248.

[3]*The Loci Communes of Philip Melanchthon,* Boston: Meador Publishing Company, 1944.

selves just how far Melanchthon has departed from the so-called
pure Lutheranism.

It is my hope that these works in their new English garb will
serve further to introduce my readers to the real spirit and thought
of Melanchthon rather than their having to rely on the secondary
accounts of him in works on church history and compendia of
dogma and of doctrine. Only by a direct communion with Melanchthon's own spirit can one be in a position to evaluate fairly the
large role which he played in the formation and direction of the
course of the Protestant Reformation. If I can serve the church in
this small office of placing this great teacher of the church in more
proper historical perspective, then the tedious and exacting hours
of translation under great administrative pressure and tension will
be more than rewarded by a great sense of joy.

I must express my thanks to Miss Altha Brown, assistant to the
Registrar of Wilberforce University, for her careful work on the
manuscript. Likewise, I owe a debt of gratitude to Dean E. E.
Flack of Hamma Divinity School for his constant encouragement
of my researches into Melanchthon and for many specific good
offices rendered from time to time. Finally, I must express my thanks
to my wife, Rosalie, whose constant devotion, tenderness, and kindly
love have been the chief factors which have inspired me in the
midst of my investigations.

CHARLES LEANDER HILL

Wilberforce University
Wilberforce, Ohio

CONTENTS

Luther took special notice of these theses and praised them highly in a letter addressed to Staupitz in 1519. Both Melanchthon and Luther had developed a great interest in the dogma of transubstantiation and had criticized it on the basis of the norm of Scripture. Theses 16-18 were especially noteworthy. These provoked serious comments from John Eck, who wrote down his impressions and sent them to the princes.

CHAPTER ONE

BACCALAUREATE THESES

Delivered September 1519

Peter Fontanus, Dean of Theology, will discuss the propositions submitted, and Philip Melanchthon will reply.

1. Human nature loves itself chiefly for its own sake.

2. It cannot love God for his own sake.

3. Both divine law and natural law have decreed that God must be loved for his own sake.

4. Since we cannot do this, the Law is the reason we fear God in a servile manner.

5. We must hate what we fear.

6. The Law, therefore, causes us even to hate God.

7. Just as hate is not the beginning of love, so servile fear is not the beginning of filial fear.

8. It follows that servile fear is not the beginning of repentance.

9. Therefore the gracious act of Christ is righteousness.

10. All of our righteousness is a gracious imputation of God.

11. Therefore it is true that even good works are sins.

12. The intellect can give assent to no given proposition without reason or experience.

13. Nor can the will by itself force the intellect to give assent.

14. The will, drawn away by love to an object of faith, orders the intellect to give assent.

15. This assent is faith or wisdom.

16. It is not necessary for a Catholic to believe any other articles of faith than those to which Scripture is a witness.

17. The authority of councils is below the authority of Scripture.

18. Therefore not to believe in the *"character indelibilis,"* transubstantiation, and the like is not open to the charge of heresy.

19. Faith acquired is mere opinion.

20. He who fails in one point is guilty of all.

21. The Commandments teach us to love our enemy, not to take revenge, not to swear an oath, but to have things in common.

22. The laws of nature are the qualities with which the soul is created.

23. Human nature strives for well being *(bene esse)* more than it strives simply to exist *(esse)*.

24. There is one God in the divine categories, and he is the sum of all things.

Melanchthon accompanied Luther to the Leipzig Disputation.[1] They entered Leipzig on June 24, 1519, and took up abode in the home of Melchior Lotther, a printer. The debate between Eck and Carlstadt began on June 27. Luther made his first appearance on July 4, 1519.[2] On the basis of Luther's thirteenth thesis Eck and Luther entered into debate on the question of the divine right of papal authority. This phase of the debate drove Luther to an even deeper conception of the church. On July 15 the disputation was closed so that the acts might be placed before the faculties of the universities of Erfurt and Paris for decision.

On July 21 Melanchthon wrote his report on the debate to his friend John Oecolampadius of Tübingen. Eight days later he wrote Spalatin that he had sent this report to the press. It is not at all surprising that this report was on the lips of everyone. It did not disturb Melanchthon that the decision of the faculties of Erfurt and Paris had not been made known.

❈   ❈   ❈

During the same interval the Benedictine scholar Matthew Hiscold from the cloister in Bosau wrote his "Epistola de Lipsica Disputatione" to Frederick the Wise, and H. Emser also wrote his "Epistola de Disputatione Lipsicense."[3]

For footnotes see pages 187-188.

LETTER ON THE LEIPZIG DEBATE
1519

**To the theologian John Oecolampadius, Philip
Melanchthon sends greetings in Christ.**

I do not think it important, nor do you especially desire, that I
express with many words my affection and good will toward you.
For that most excellent spirit of sincere love has united our souls
so auspiciously that I hope our friendship cannot be shaken by any
exigency in the midst of the vicissitudes of all human affairs nor
that it will strike deeper roots by those common, favor-seeking
approbations found in that type of letter by which friendships are
scarcely nourished. It is equally incumbent upon both of our spirits
that a friendship be not entered into at any time in the spirit of
jealousy or with such trifling blandishments. Would that I could
with grateful heart acknowledge the kindness of that one who has
joined such a friend to me, not with Thesean but with Christian
faith! For, to be sure, there is no mortal man whose beneficence
ever since my youth has been more constant for me than yours; this
has been shown in a truly liberal way, bringing about "the marriage
of the graces." For our interests did not permit my kindness to
match yours. Since in bestowing favors you excel, I beseech you,
grant me to conquer in loving.

Aristotle is of the opinion that he who has bestowed a benefit
upon another is to be loved by the other only as much as the benefit
deserves, or certainly for the sake of the benefit. He argues subtly
but not altogether rightly. As far as I am concerned the goal of our
love is not any benefit from you, but the author of our friendship,
the spirit of Christ. Meanwhile, whatever good you have done for a
friend, you were obligated by the common right of charity; I, in

turn, in your name shall not shirk my duty if at any time the occasion arises.

On now to what concerns me. Since we have nearly all our literary pursuits in common, I was unwilling for you to be frustrated by those things which have been done with greater expectation than is in keeping with the affair at Leipzig, in my opinion—things which concern certain ambiguous topics of the theologians. I think you are concerned, for you are not only playing your role with dignity among the theologians in the Swabian theater Augsburg, but you are also striving that theological literature be taught purely and simply. Indeed, this province of debate was first undertaken for no other reason than that it might be made known openly what a great difference there is between the old theology, that of Christ, and the new, Aristotelian doctrine. But what has come about or the direction toward which matters have inclined is certainly not easy for me to determine. Therefore I shall more diligently follow all things that pertain to this cause, that you may be able more discerningly to derive something certain from them. Doubtlessly a diverse report will reach you in which, by reference to the historic faith and by means of the headings of the discussion expressed as simply as possible, I shall enable you to understand what and concerning what the controversy is.

And now to begin with something of an outline: Last year the views about indulgences which Martin set forth for dispute were marked with obelisks by Eck. He wrote with too much bitterness for me to bring up here. In his conclusions, which are available, Carlstadt removed some of the obelisks. Eck then replied to Carlstadt with a defense, in which he said many things in a milder manner than he had done in his obelisks. Carlstadt refuted Eck's defense by bringing forth a small book. Long was the violence and long the digressions. To pass over other things, it was finally decided to debate the issues, and a day was set.

John Eck of Ingolstadt and Andrew Carlstadt and Martin Luther of Wittenberg met together at Leipzig. A summary of the facts had been compressed into very brief conclusions so that just what was to be debated might be the more clearly set forth. I believe that what was agreed upon as to the conduct of the debate is sufficiently clear to you: that the case was to be carried out with the help of secretaries taking notes in shorthand, that this written document was to be published, and that the proceedings were to be in the possession of all of the ablest men. First Eck talked with those who had been designated overseers of the debate by the illustrious Prince George, Duke of Saxony, the patron of humanistic studies. Eck had given notice that it seemed to him to be the right of the debaters that it not be recorded that the increasing power of those who assembled to fight was gradually subsiding because of delays due to recording or that their spirits were bolstered by the attack but waned because of delay. I do not know whether this can arise from theological honesty, in which nothing is so important as the impression that nothing is said in attack, or rashly, or with an unrestrained spirit. In literary pursuits, especially in the matter of piety, I feel there is nothing either more important or more salutary than the friendly meeting of learned and good men, where opinion is compared with opinion by placid and tranquil minds, least given to obstinacy, where it is not disgraceful to be defeated nor praiseworthy to defeat. Thus I think that there is scarcely anything more dangerous than those popular arguments wherein the concern for victory cannot but detract from whatever good there may be. You know how many prudent things have been written about this opinion by Nazianzen and likewise by our Erasmus. But it had already been agreed concerning the secretaries, for Carlstadt could not be persuaded otherwise. As soon as the contest was undertaken, and Eck wished certain judges also to be designated, Carlstadt did not refuse.

So on the twenty-seventh day of June John Eck and Carlstadt met. The subject of their debate was free will *(arbitrium)*—whether any good work is by our own free choice; that is, as they themselves express it, whether or not we properly *(de congruo)* merit grace when we do that which is in our own power—I am using their very words. Although this should have been the subject for discussion, see how far they were carried away in their dispute and upon what rocks they dashed themselves. It should have been a debate on what our will *(voluntas)* can do of itself without grace. They carried the question into an altogether different direction and disputed four whole days, I believe, on this: whether the will *(voluntas)* only receives a good work and grace alone performs the good work itself. Into these Symplegades they forced a discussion which was not so very necessary and which was quite different from that begun by Carlstadt. Eck conceded that there is no genuine power in our will *(voluntas)* by which it may produce a good work, but there is only receptivity, the receptivity wrought by grace. This is what Eck seemed at first to oppose.

Then Carlstadt asked him if he would grant that the total good work is done by God, and he replied that the total work was done by God but not totally. See how astute this comment is, how worthy to be dignified by the name of theology; today anyone is free to multiply words to the third power.

At first Eck confessed that the will (*voluntas*) is moved by God, and then he said that it is in our power to agree. This was countered by Carlstadt with several citations from Augustine and especially the one from Paul which reads: "For God is at work in you, both to will and to work for his good pleasure" (Phil. 2:13 RSV). And if I am not mistaken, this proposition was established by Carlstadt. Eck had transcribed from Bernard several things in defense of his dogma, but they were largely irrelevant to the subject. These are almost all the arguments Eck had with Carlstadt. We wasted, I believe, a full good week in these matters, the outlines of which I have noted for you in a concise manner. I first learned with these men as teachers what is the meaning of that which the ancients called "arguing like a Sophist." It is astonishing with what an uproar and how sadly all of these things have been treated and just as astonishing how little has been accomplished. For the Spirit loves his moments of repose in which he penetrates our hearts and takes possession of us in a manner most eager, not for glory, but for ascertaining the truth. That spouse, beloved of Christ, does not stand forth in the doorway, but leads her spouse into the house of her mother. Neither do any rays of celestial wisdom shine forth through us unless beforehand we have been purified by the cross and are "dead to the basic elements of the world," to use Paul's language.

At this Martin also descended into the arena, for up to this time it was not quite certain that he would engage in the controversy, since he could not well designate any judges of the insidious affair and retain his right to appeal. Nevertheless, when it had been agreed that he speak, they began to discuss the authority of the Roman pontiff, and the controversy was about whether the authority of an ecumenical pontiff could be proved by divine right. Martin frankly confessed that there was an ecumenical pontiff. The dispute was about this point: whether his authority can be proved by divine right. Since in this topic the going was a little rougher, five days, if I am not mistaken, were spent in its discussion. Eck said many bitter things, many uncivil things, though all of them in a brief way, just to stir up the crowd to ill will against Martin.

Eck's first argument was that the church cannot be without a head since it is a civil body. Therefore, the pope is by divine right the head of the church. Then Martin rejoined that Christ himself is the head, and since the church is a spiritual kingdom, it needs no other head, according to Colossians 1. Eck added to these some citations from Jerome and Cyprian. Only he himself saw how much they prove about divine right. But then some citations manifestly from among the same writers were called into question, and these Eck had presented as authoritative. He boasted of the authority of Bernard's *To Eugenius*, as though it were the panoply of Achilles, yet in the very same book, *To Eugenius*, there are statements which in some respects support Martin's position. On the other hand, who is so stupid that he does not understand what we owe Bernard in this affair? He used a passage from Matthew's Gospel: "Thou art Peter, and on this rock . . ." (Matt. 16:18). Now Martin interpreted this to be a confession of faith and held that Peter, in this place, is playing the part of the universal church, while Christ is calling himself the rock *(petra)*. And he demonstrated this with many reasonable inferences from the order of the sentence itself. Eck likewise used the passage "Feed my sheep . . ." (John 21:17), a thing said personally and privately to Peter. Martin answered that equal authority was afterwards handed down to all the apostles in these words: "Receive [*accipite* (plural)] the Holy Spirit. If you [plural] forgive [*remiseritis*] the sins of any . . ." (John 20:22). For these are the words of a commissioned office, and Christ taught what it means to feed and what sort of person he wants to feed the sheep.

Against these statements Eck asserted the authority of the Council of Constance, which among the condemned articles of the Hussites also included this one: It is necessary for salvation to believe that the Roman pontiff is universal. It was also boasted in various ways that a council cannot err. Wisely Martin replied that not all articles had been condemned as heretical, and he said many other things, to all of which it is irksome to refer at this time. Nor is it proper here to treat the subject of what constitutes the authority of councils. This is clear: A council cannot institute new articles of faith. Because of this Martin unfortunately granted that it seemed that he was opposing the councils, although he maintained nothing with any greater reverence than that councils should possess their own authority. Then charges of heresy, Bohemian factions, and other accusations of that nature were thrown up against him. Eck granted that the authority of all the apostles had been equal, but that it does not follow that bishops are of equal power. For there is a difference between the office of an apostle and administration. Apostleship is nothing but the sending of an ambassador "for obedience of the faith," as Paul says in Romans. I do not see what difference there is between apostleship and administration. It seemed intolerable to Eck for anyone anywhere to depart from the decrees of the pontiffs or from any words whatsoever of any of the holy fathers. But Martin supported his view about the pontificate by a passage in Galatians (2:6), which was in accord with him, as far as I can see: "And from those who were reputed to be something (what they were makes no difference to me; God shows no partiality)—those, I say, who were of repute added nothing to me." In the meantime Eck expressed the opinion that the apostles had been selected by Christ but the bishops had been ordained by Peter. From this you may judge the remainder for yourself. When asked whether the Roman pontiff is not named a "Universal Bishop" according to the constitution which is reckoned among the decrees, he replied that he must not be called "Universal Bishop" but "Bishop of the Universal Church."

After this the question was about purgatory, the scope of which I do not think was even touched upon. For although it was to be discussed what power the pope had over purgatory, Eck began another song as to how he could prove the existence of purgatory. This is too widely accepted to necessitate its being discussed so often in the schools. The usual passage in Maccabees was used by Eck to defend his view. In the argument it seemed to Martin that according to the position of Jerome the Book of Maccabees was not valid. On the other hand, Eck contended that we ought to attribute as much validity to the Book of Maccabees as to the Gospel, an opinion worthy, to be sure, of a theologian, and he held firmly to this view. He added the passage of Paul in First Corinthians: "He himself will be saved, but only as through fire" (1 Cor. 3:15). Concerning this passage you know how interpreters differ. He cited also that passage in Matthew: "Make friends quickly with your accuser . . ." (Matt. 5:25), which speaks also about a prison "till you have paid the last penny" (Matt. 5:26). This passage he distorted, as you see, disregarding its context and occasion. It is wrong to think that the prison in that passage is to be understood as meaning purgatory. Would that the people of Christ were more fortunately instructed than by interpretations of that nature. For the most part they lead Scripture too far from its sources to retain its natural force. Furthermore, he also brought forth in the interest of purgatory this passage in the Psalm: "We went through fire and through water" (Ps. 66:12), and I know not what else he cited with equal confidence.

There was a lesser dispute waged about indulgences. I should rather say that they produced a joke and sport for Eck himself. At last they discussed repentance. And I do not know whether Eck's reflections came to grips with the scope of this question, but they did demonstrate certain penalties for satisfaction, which Martin admitted. But that divine righteousness demands that a person repent for individual sins in accordance with individual penalties that are in the power of man to remit was not apparent to me from those methods of reasoning. These are the principal matters that came up in that entire debate. Many other things are too ridiculous for me to load them on you who are more happily occupied in some other way.

The remaining two days were given over to Carlstadt. On the first, they discussed the wall, as they call it, of grace. Eck conceded that it is broken down not by nature but by grace. On the second day they debated whether we sin in any good work whatsoever. Concerning this both Eck and Carlstadt contended by using a great many illustrious passages of Scripture. The seventh chapter of Paul's Letter to the Romans seemed to me to support somewhat Carlstadt's view.

As I was about to write more I was called elsewhere to necessary duties. Although I have perhaps already written too much, yet it has pleased me to talk some nonsense with you, my very dear friend, and that, too, about a matter which I myself saw was being conducted with greater expectation than results.

What others think about praiseworthy debates of this kind I do not know, but to me they seem indeed to be without Christian relevance. In this theater of action these men displayed natural abilities, diverse knowledge, and manifold learning, and from these I would hope that there might come a very great addition to piety. But to me Eck seemed to be greatly admired by very many because of his diverse and outstanding natural gifts. You have become acquainted with Carlstadt, I believe, from his writings. He is a good man of rare knowledge and plainly learned somewhat beyond the ordinary. I admire the vivacious disposition and also the erudition and eloquence in Martin, who has been known to me in

an intimate way by long association. I cannot but love dearly his
sincere and purely Christian spirit.

Extend a greeting from me to our mutual friends. You know what
the Greeks say: "In war many things are empty." Therefore do not
believe all the things which you hear about the outcome of this debate and of its fame nor all of the things which you hear about
those who strove for fame in it. Farewell.

Wittenberg, July 21

In accordance with the statutes of the University of Wittenberg, each year on the Day of the Conversion of Paul a festival celebration took place. Paul was considered the patron of the theological faculty. On January 25, 1520, the Elector and Jerome Brunner, who had been sent by the emperor and who had come from a session of the diet, attended the festival.[1]

In his address on this occasion Melanchthon treated the differences between Pauline and Scholastic theology. He stood under the influences of the newly discovered Paul and praised highly his theology, in which one can find full salvation. Everything, he taught, depends on the "beneficium Christi," through which peace of conscience is to be won. The address did not satisfy him entirely, but it made strong impressions on those who were present to hear it. It was immediately put into print.[2]

At the wish of the Palace, Melanchthon had to dedicate the writing to the person who had been sent by the emperor, whereas he had intended to dedicate it originally to his friend John Hess of Breslau. In order not to disappoint Hess completely Melanchthon appended to this work an open letter as a sort of postscript to this publication.[3]

CHAPTER THREE

PAUL AND THE SCHOLASTICS
1520

To Doctor Jerome Brunner, confidential advisor of the late Charles Caesar Augustus, greeting from Philip Melanchthon.

In accordance with the custom of our Academy, we celebrated very recently the annual day of Saint Paul with an oration of some sort. This address, Jerome, I am sending to you, in the first place, because far and wide you have praised men of letters, and to the same degree letters also in such a praiseworthy manner that, by way of our thanks, as many of us as profess letters owe our studies to you; and, in the second place, because at the time of which I have spoken, you happened by good fortune to be present at Wittenberg together with the most illustrious prince, blessed Frederick, Duke Elector of Saxony, a hero worthy of the memory of all ages. You were there as the legate of blessed Charles Caesar. Even this one reason would dedicate this discourse to you. For since, following a public custom which now has nearly the force of law, men of letters commonly dedicate their studies to the legates of kings, it is right for me also to bear witness in some honorable manner to my obligation to you. Accordingly, this address, into which by chance you have fallen, I am now dedicating to you, and that, too, as one who loves letters.

If in this address there is nothing else of which the learned shall approve, you certainly, with the dexterity and the candor characteristic of you, will approve of my zeal. Doubtless your great worth was deserving of fuller considerations. But you will interpret favorably what fortune has given. A fact that is of consequence to my argument is that the oration needs a patron. For I have spoken

about the theology of Paul and against the dangerous schools
of the theologians of our age, in opposition to which there is need
of more than one Hercules, so to speak. Therefore you will undertake the patronage not only of my oration, but the patronage of
the Scriptures in general, a cause for which I have labored, and
one which is certainly worthy of your name. For it is an illustrious
thing to safeguard letters, as well as a pious thing to vindicate the
Scriptures. Martin Luther, a man equally pious and learned and
one who is truly a theologian, I do commend to you. Farewell.

Wittenberg in Saxony, 1520.

On the Festival of the Apostle Paul

We are now celebrating a festival for the blessed Apostle Paul.
How more fitting to dedicate this than in festive praise of that great
man, and moreover of the heavenly blessings which have been
scattered abroad throughout the whole world through him, a
chosen instrument to be sure! For what is rarer than a Paul? What
more marvelous example is there of divine goodness? For upon
him divine goodness, with a most generous heart, lavished nothing
but the very best gifts. But the opportunities for speaking are fewer
than the proper consideration of so grave and weighty an argument
demands. Furthermore, in view of my own weakness, it would have
been easier for me to admire and to adore the tremendous gifts of
Paul with a reverent mind than to set them forth in an oration. Indeed I see in him something altogether more august than can be
expressed in human words. For although there are things which he
has in common with others—esteem for his fatherland; contempt
for pleasure, wealth, glory; cold, sun, calumnies, hunger, wounds,
pain—still, in some manner which I do not understand, these
appear to me to be greater in Paul than they commonly are in
others. This is true because the same Spirit imparts himself in such
various ways to many that the same natural quality in all is not of
the same force. And, as in the case of many jewels which have one
color when set in gold but another when set in silver, so each man's
style of life is in accord with the individual powers of each. Therefore I think it improper to extol Paul with ordinary praises, since
in him there is nothing ordinary to detect. It is evident that the
power of the highest love was attained by this one man beyond any
other, in that he wished himself to be cursed by Christ to save his
own nation. His incomparable trust is also obvious in that he denied

that any force, whether of men or of angels or of devils, could ever wrench him away from Christ. He had a knowledge of hidden things; snatched right up into the third heaven, he heard certain secret things of which even he himself could not speak. He had such contempt for life that he counted death as gain, and further such contempt for that gain (for he would rise from death) that although death was far more desirable than life itself, he nevertheless preferred to live in order to fulfill his ministry. Such was the grandeur of his doctrine that in this enterprise he outstripped the whole company of the apostles. He was a man of superb courage, as seen in his opposition even to the highest authorities among the apostles, James and Peter, in order to proclaim grace. As for such qualities as these—and I have enumerated only a few out of the innumerable list—since they belong in a special way to Paul, who, besides perhaps Paul himself, could do justice to them in an oration? Among them indeed, as I contend, first place goes to doctrine. For other adornments he himself enjoyed privately, but the enjoyment of his doctrine is ours.

It seems best at this time, when it is not permissible to use many words, to exhort you to embrace this doctrine with faithful zeal. In order for me to do this, there are many other reasons, but particularly this one, responsible for my not having examined Paul more closely from any other source than from his own letters: One's own speech is one's own best revealer. It would not seem fitting for any praise to be taken from Paul's character through any fault of mine; therefore I think it very satisfactory for these festive days if I shall have induced our youth in some manner to meditate upon the doctrine of this wisest hero. For I am of the opinion that Christ, and therefore the sum of our salvation, cannot be known so accurately from the writings of anyone else, or from the commentaries of any other, as they can from those of Paul. No oration can commend Paul more efficaciously to the human race than this praise. For although other reasons call each person to his own pursuits, hither, to be sure, necessity equally draws all.

Some of the arts are learned for the sake of the mind but not by all sorts of persons; some are joined to the profit that will be gained, and to be ignorant of these is really of no consequence. On the contrary, it is sometimes even better not to have learned them. But those arts which show the way of salvation, a plan of absolute happiness, these indeed are the ones which all rightly ought to seek out. Philosophy should be sought—and by this term all an-

tiquity especially has been included—in order that from that source
one may seek a form of the better life. By the consensus of all the
wise, the very best kind of discipline has always been considered
to be that most adapted to the improvement of character and the
pursuits of life. In this connection I shall show just what we who
have been washed in the blood of Christ actually owe to Paul. It
is not right for Christians to seek a form or plan of life from philosophers but from the divine books. Among these, just what parts
are Paul's, I shall point out to you, if it is not burdensome for you
to hear.

Among the number of divine books some reveal laws; others,
examples of life and character; others, dim prophecies about Christ;
and still others, the great deeds of Christ. But who explains in a
more weighty, accurate, and full manner than Paul the blessing
which Christ by his own blood has brought to the entire world?
There is some value for living to have laws, for they make it possible to know what is fitting and what is not. There is some value,
likewise, in seeing examples before our eyes which add a spur for
the embracing of virtue. There is some value in remembering the
achievements of Christ, certainly the exemplar of absolute virtue.
But it is of the highest value by far to know what is Christ's true
glory, why he came down to this earth, and just what the incarnation of the eternal Word brings into the world. For therein has been
placed the very essence of salvation. Laws prescribe the beauty of
integrity and set forth examples, especially that archetype Christ.
But the grace of Christ, which has been declared to the whole world
by the Gospel of Paul, is imparted to the whole human race. Laws
and examples simply adumbrate virtue, but the grace of Christ,
which Paul preaches, absolves from sin.

Now, just as for conquering it is not enough for a soldier simply
to know by what skills he must contend with the enemy, if courage
and physical powers are absent, so is it not enough for living to
possess laws or examples well and beautifully, unless one is prepared in mind *(animus)* to obey those laws. Whence you may seek
this very mind is not adequately taught either by laws or by examples, but by Paul. The Gentiles were by no means lacking in
laws for good living, nor in good examples, but they lacked someone to teach them from what source they must seek that mind by
which they might be reconciled to their laws. It was of great
importance that to the laws promulgated by Moses, and to the
declarations of the prophets, and to the histories, the Letters of

Paul were added; in them the grace of our Savior is described, and in them is shown from what source, once and for all, absolute happiness should be sought. For this is the scope of Paul's wisdom, this is the very sum. As for the rest, he gives exhortations *(paraineseis)* and lays down various laws for living, and this is what he has in common with other sacred writers.

But in a peculiar and special way we learn from Paul the very nature and power of Christ's grace, and this praise we properly owe to him. Humanly speaking, no writers have deserved more praise than those who have set down in letters the mercy of Christ, lest a compendium of our salvation be not known and lest oblivion of God's goodness and their own obligations carry away unmindful mortals.

To be sure, to know Christ consists not only in possessing a knowledge of his mighty acts but in embracing his grace with a thankful mind; for this grace through Christ himself has been disseminated throughout the whole world by the heavenly Father, and by him alone distinction is made between the ungodly Gentiles and truly Christian souls. Nor has any divine plan commended this unto us more powerfully than the memory of that which comes through Christ, by far his greatest act of grace. Moreover, just what the nature of this gracious act is it seems that I must explain in a few words, lest you be ignorant of just what we owe to Christ and what we owe to Paul, the herald of Christ.

As God at various times and in various ways has declared his own goodness (as it is also commonly said that all things are full of Jove), so he has expressed his goodness in a most absolute manner in Christ by whom in extraordinary fashion he has snatched mankind from the very jaws of Orcus. For as many as are born of Adam are born children of wrath and of death; and being wretched because of our nature, we are so dragged away to vices that by no counsel of our own, by no powers of our own can we be called back from them. A manifold cupidity exercises its tyranny over us. Each in accordance with his own lust is carried away, one in one way, another in another. There is strife going on, whether occasioned by reason or by law; in our unhappy state we carry on perpetual war with ourselves. I do not quite know whether the scourges of conscience in that condition, and the terrible evils there are in death can be rightly expressed. Certainly they are of such a kind that even certain wise men have thought that it is best not to be born.

Therefore God Most Great, Most Good has sent to the earth his Son, clothed in our flesh, by whom he might be both closer and more lovable, through whom the kingdom of sin and of death might once and for all be destroyed and in order that law and reason and desire might be brought into conformity therewith. Finally God sent his Son that through him peace and life might be planted in the souls of all those who would accommodate themselves to him through faith.

Therefore we are indebted to Christ for the spirit of absolute virtue and peace, or, to say it in Greek, he is the author of happiness (*euthumia*), and, what is more, of absolute happiness. How great these blessings are he will estimate who compares them with the evils of the human race among the Gentiles. Even the philosophers have posited blessedness in absolute virtue and perpetual tranquillity of soul, and without doubt all human reason concurs in the same; but the source of such a heart (*animus*), the philosophers did not seem to see, and this is the very mystery that was hidden for so many ages, the grace of Christ. The only harbor for human misery is Christ, and whether the serious sickness of the flesh, or conscience, or the fear of death disturbs, the ready remedy is from the grace of Christ. That is true unless one thinks that Christ spoke these words in vain: "Come to me, all who labor and are heavy laden, and I will give you rest." He rejoices to be called a Savior, not a judge, who came down in the flesh, took upon himself the form of worthless humanity, and from the power of sin or of the flesh, the tyranny of the law, and the more than cruel kingdom of death he has so liberated the human race that he will forever be with all of those who have fled to his banners.

Those patriarchs who were saved knew about the grace of Christ from certain secret prophecies, for they could not have been saved if they had not been liberated by the generous help of Christ. The prophets, too, sing the same song, a hymn of peace and a pean of the new sabbath. That illustrious Baptist taught the same, he than whom, according to Christ's word, there was none greater, who pointed with his finger to the Savior and called him a lamb, upon whom the evils of the whole human race were heaped.

The apostles proclaimed the same thing and especially our Paul, who, there is no doubt, was designated as the herald of Christian grace unto the Gentiles, just as the Baptist was once the herald to the Jewish people. Up to the time of Christ the Jewish people were devoid of the authority of pardon and the forgiveness of transgression; and how bitter a thing this was to anxious minds, I leave you to judge for yourself. John was the first to point out publicly the author of pardon and the victim through whom we would be reconciled with the most high God; he did this when he said: "Behold the Lamb of God, behold him who takes away sins." Up to this point Judea had possessed the law, but from whom it should seek dispositions that loved the law and from whom it should seek the love of virtue was first declared by John when he testified that he baptized with water but that Christ would baptize with the Holy Spirit. He baptizes with water who prescribes the law and who adumbrates virtue with words. But he baptizes with the Holy Spirit who imbues our hearts with the Spirit and who frees us from all the mathematics of our own virtues. For laws, however right their admonitions may be, cannot effect this in our souls, that it may not be agreeable for evils to exist, that virtue may not be hated.

It is quite agreed that wicked Gentiles were without pardon for their crimes and that perchance they denied that they lacked absolute virtue. Among them there were, strange to say, some philosophers, whom I should like to examine more closely in this very matter. Plato in his *Laws*, when he locates happiness in virtue, denies that that is happiness which is not most pleasing and confesses that this sweetness itself is removed from virtue. There cannot exist absolute virtue unless the same is most pleasing. Likewise, elsewhere he calls a tyrant over law that which is opposed to the genius and capacity of nature. Should we call absolute virtue that with which natural pleasure does not agree? Or which example of the virtues have the poets and philosophers set forth, in which it is not possible to detect some remaining trace of vice?

Therefore it is by the grace of Christ alone that we have pardon for transgressions as well as the Spirit of absolute virtue and the Author of peace, to whom the prophets pointed with obscure prophecies and whom Paul once preached to Gentiles and Jews, and whom it has been granted in our times to know from the letters of one man: Paul.

I have set forth in a few words the nature of Christ's grace, of which Paul serves as the herald. For both peace of conscience and absolute virtue were unknown before the incarnation of Christ, to the Jews as well as to the Gentiles.

The other sacred writers also have ever been mindful of this grace, but not clearly enough to be understood unless Paul had illuminated the whole argument by so many epistles and disputations. With what rhetorical figures, what flowers and ornaments of speech he captivates the reader in his works I can by no means express in words. Alcibiades attributed to the conversations of Socrates a certain calculated energy, as did Socrates to those of Lysias, the ancient comedy to those of Pericles, the poet Homer to those of Ulysses, and unless conjecture deceives me, that is about what *molu* signifies. But by how many feet are these surpassed by our Paul, whom even the Gentiles in their admiration called Mercury. In my case, to be sure, after I surrendered my mind to him to be shaped, I know full well what he has done. And would that all would prefer to try this out for themselves rather than put confidence merely in my words. As a boy I did some damage to my mind in preoccupation with the literature of the philosophers, which, I hope, the doctrine of Paul some day will repair. For according to my judgment those who think that the affairs of the Christian life are aided by philosophical literature are entirely wrong. For Christian doctrine alone is efficacious for inciting and inspiring our hearts, a thing which the apostles confessed when they called the philosophy of Christ the word of eternal life; Christ alone is the life and the truth and the light and the way. On the contrary, the opinions of men they called death, mendacity, darkness, and error. What madness is it, therefore, what blindness, since the Scriptures alone point out a succinct way of salvation, if you seek the beauty and structure of virtue from the clever thoughts of philosophers when they are obsolete!

Philosophy prescribes laws for living, but the heavenly Father prescribes much more holy ones. Since philosophy, to be sure, does not yet know exactly the very genius of man, how can it avoid faults by laws? Philosophy teaches that virtue comes by practice and habit, but with natural feelings opposing, do we still not see that nothing is accomplished by practice? For just as an ape is always an ape, even though clothed in purple, by the same token one will not conquer sickness of the soul by any counsel or any art.

But the ancient philosophers in a great contention disputed whether character had more importance in establishing virtue than did discipline, practice, and experience. Nor has anyone been discovered up till now who has not affirmed that nature without discipline has much value, but discipline without nature has very little. Wherefore there is need for some other teacher of souls, obviously the heavenly Spirit, to seize the innermost hearts of men, to renew, inspire, take possession of, enkindle, and transform them.

For the virtue that is gained by human exertion is masked and is plainly playing the role of some preposterous silenus, replendent in outer appearance, but if you should examine it, you would discover nothing but the foulest of passions. A sewer of such a nature is the mind of man, on every side festering with all the most poisonous passions. Even the Platonists saw that the minds of men needed a certain internal catharsis, as they called it, that is, a cleansing, without which they denied that solid virtue could be established. But when should we seek this catharsis? Hear Paul, who writes that Christ for this very thing came into the world, so that, if anyone should throw himself upon him, he would bestow the living Spirit, even the creator of virtue. For what else does Paul do when he discourses about the ancient law but teach that our minds are improved and set at peace by no exercise of our own?

The law was handed down to teach the right, but Christ bestows his Spirit, who absolves us from what the law demands and so imbues us mortals with a certain celestial pleasure and moistens us with some divine nectar, that whatever is foreign to law becomes bitter, foul, and detestable. If there are some of this disposition, Paul indeed denies that the law was given for them, that is for those who of their own accord have embraced virtue so that it is not necessary to force them to do so. For there is no need to put the spur to a horse that has been given loose reins. Likewise Paul does this when he compares the realm of sin and of law with the realm of love. For it is not within our power to drive away from their own kingdom the passions of sin which occupy an abode deep within the soul like some impregnable fortress where they exercise their tyranny over all our members. Therefore, since there is nothing superior to or more powerful than false esteem to establish tyranny, by what attractions do they not capture and subjugate the stomach, tongue, and eyes, and finally the mind itself? Some of the ancients thought that reason in man functions like a charioteer and called the passions horses. But reason is conquered by passion. Holding the reins in vain, the charioteer is borne on by the horses. Nor does the team heed curb. Rather the passions shake off reason in the same way that the horses of the sun's chariot did Phaethon. This power of sin is conquered by the grace of Christ alone.

Paul makes the same point when he compares the spirit of love with the spirit of fear. For that mind is servile which is forced by fear to do its duty. Far from calling fear the source of virtue, we are agreed that it does not even liberate for vice. On the contrary, we owe the perfection of virtue of an upright man to love, which plainly is something of a foretaste of divine goodness. The same thing Paul does when he discourses about the letter as the author of death and the Spirit as the giver of life. For the letter is a rough sketch *(skiographia)* of virtue, that is law, by which both the philosophers and the dregs of philosophers, the scholastic theologians of our age, think that the minds of men are excited to the pursuit of virtue. What dreams! How much more truly does Paul teach that human souls are terrified and slain by the law, but made alive by the Spirit of Christ. For as the character of man bears with indignation the fact that it is not permitted his burning lust to relax the reins, so when the law forbids it, the law also must be regarded as an object of hate. But by means of the Spirit of Christ it is brought about that it is not pleasant even if it be permitted to indulge a desire. But I ask, what human philosophy, what practice and exercises have caused the one who seems so agreeable to the flesh not to enjoy the fruits of desire? In what manner does virtue become as pleasing to us as vice is to the flesh? This certainly is a new world, to which not only life, glory, and pleasure have become bitter, but also whatever there is toward which our flesh is borne headlong.

Whence we may seek such a world as this, such a spirit and such a disposition, Paul himself indicates, when, with the law rejected and the kingdom of sin and of law destroyed, he describes for us the kingdom of grace and of peace. Almost all of the rest of the sacred books instruct us in laws. But Paul—since it is agreed that human minds by nature abhor laws—sets before our mortal eyes the Christ, from whom we obtain the Spirit of virtue and the author of peace.

And this is the succinct way to blessedness, not through philosophy, not through sacred laws, but through Christ. Philosophy is in error; our minds are not equal to divine laws. But the Spirit of Christ reveals that which is ordered by divine laws. Therefore, if your salvation is a matter of your heart, if to know Christ and Christ's grace is your real concern, take into your hands finally the divine books of Paul and delight yourselves with celestial wisdom. Let both urge our youth toward this: an age which has been exposed to some dangers and also the customs of this very corrupt time, in which it is of supreme importance by which opinions and by what kind of teachers their rude minds are being fashioned. For in what is commonly thought, namely, that young people can be excited to the pursuit and love of virtue by profane letters, I fear that we are deceiving ourselves.

On the other hand, there is a certain force in divine letters that is to be admired, for by it zealous minds are carried away and enkindled, and never would you know the hand of the gods to be more present, as they say, than in sacred language. And in this Paul is even more apt for shaping character because not only does he prescribe laws for living, but he also reveals Christ, from whom you may obtain, from whose wounds you may drink up, the spirit of virtues.

With what great damage the schools of theology have neglected Paul up to now, I shudder to say. For after having condemned the doctrine of Paul, they embraced Aristotle, and scarcely is the name of Christ left. Certainly his grace is unknown, and it is from this alone that his divinity can properly be learned. The gods of the Gentiles were indebted to human beneficence, each god having his own class, each his own number, each his own tribe. And each was just as great as he seemed to foolish mortals to be. But the ungrateful gods were repaying this interest of men with no blessing, but with that which was both uncivil and inhuman, by no means divine.

But that of Christ is truly a divine grace, so that when he liberally pours out all of his good things upon us, he loves to be known more, actually, that he may favor than that he may be loved. O truly inestimable goodness! And what other people is there anywhere that has gods drawing near them as our God is present in all of our supplications? He who takes away from our midst this grace of Christ takes away Christ; and no more detestable blasphemy than this can be spoken.

On the other hand, no worship is more pleasing to Christ than to embrace this goodness of his with pious zeal. In this one respect we Christians distinguish ourselves from the Gentiles and the Jews: Before our eyes we have Christ, who bestows the Spirit upon his own, who is both a pledge and the author of virtues. Those who teach men to secure comfort for their fearful consciences from any other source desecrate him. The same is true of those who teach that strength for souls that have been badly afflicted is to be gained elsewhere. And these are truly the ones who attack the Holy Spirit, an act of blasphemy which will not be forgiven either in this age or in the age that is to come. The future kingdom of the coming Christ was celebrated in song with more than heroic words by the prophets, as some sort of perpetual triumph of righteousness and peace. Of this kingdom and of these triumphs the schools are ignorant, as in wretched ways they torment afflicted consciences by means of their summas. Not only do they not relieve the vicious passions with their frivolous and trifling disputations, but they even add sickness to sickness, particularly since they consider many vicious passions to be virtues.

There are chiefly two blessings that commend Christ unto the world: a conscience at peace and a mind in control of the passions. Both of these have been neglected by the schools of theologians of our times, and this is something which the matter itself has clearly shown to be wrong. The Gentiles were in the habit of seeking from Mercury, success for their frauds; from Mars, fortune in military affairs; and from Juno, wealth. That we do not know what properly ought to be sought from Christ we owe to the schools, who number him almost among the gods of the stage as one who relieves sick bodies, increases family wealth, and finally as one who looks with favor on each man's most foolish desires, although he took upon himself flesh for the purpose of being present to console and strengthen the minds of men.

But why do I linger any longer in this place? How great a difference there is between the schools and the sacred doctrine of Paul they will easily discern who have, if you please, merely a passing acquaintance with him. I am not now discussing what is the nature of the discourse in the schools nor how impure and sordid is their manner of teaching and conversing, but I do warn that there is no agreement between these and Christian doctrine and that they have plainly obscured the grace of Christ. Meanwhile, to discuss what sort of things they have published with respect to the use of the Sacraments and in regard to other heavenly mysteries does not fall within the limits of this treatise. There is a common statement to the effect that a drink of water is not to be found in water which has been rendered turbid with filth. Just so no faithful man has ever satisfied his mind with scholastic theology which has become polluted by so many human arguments, nonsense, tricks, and trifling traditions. Moreover, I do not regard it as necessary to refute here the especially frivolous opinion of those who consign the doctrine of Paul to the limits of one age and who foolishly hold that it was written to Christians who were still unpolished, whereas there is now need of a more sublime theology for those fully developed. For in that age particularly there flourished both the other aspects of truly Christian wealth and especially tongues and prophecy or the interpretation of the Scriptures, since the celestial Spirit, who alone reveals the hidden mysteries of Scripture, was more familiar to their pure minds.

Perhaps the seemingly difficult speech and manner of discoursing drive away and deter some from Paul. I should like them to experience with how much less trouble they are able to follow the main point of Paul's disputations than the contentions and wicked little questions of the Schoolmen. And to say exactly what is the truth in the matter, the reason why Pauline matters are less understood is due to those excellent masters of ours who, although skilled in all of the ancient literature and correct learning, in the first place by their new interpunctuations have cut to pieces the divine language of Paul, which is both tied together by rhetorical members and compact with its own connectives. And after cutting it to pieces, they proceeded to interpret it after their fashion according to Aristotle in such a way that not even one verse anywhere agreed with any other.

In reference to these, it was not the duty of an ordinary man to trifle about the four senses in almost every individual syllable. Nor has it shamed bold men to play games in so serious a matter and in them to vie in various opinions, when no such thing ought to have been done, except when something that was both sure and very simple according to the figures of grammarians and rhetoricians should have been brought forth, as Erasmus advises in his method. Or, as the Greeks say, one thing should have been compared with another. For Scripture has not been produced in order that it may not be understood. Rather the merciful Spirit of God, who is light, did this that it might be understood in common by all the pious. Let praise depart, if any praise there be, from the philosophers of obscurity; the Spirit of God arrogates this praise to himself, in that he equally well both instructs the tender and unpolished and gives each of the most brilliant a workout.

Saint Augustine, a man of both singular genius and great experience in sacred matters, said that the apostle does not desire a man of acute understanding but only an attentive hearer. He who has been infected with the opinions of carnal philosophy does not acknowledge the wisdom of Paul. Accordingly, you will see to it that you bring to this wisdom, first, a mind that is pure, and then also one that is free from the opinions of the crowd. For unless the vase is pure, whatever you pour into it will become sour.

Antisthenes, an especially serious philosopher, speaking to a certain youth who gave himself to him for training and who asked
what things he needed in order to philosophize, said that he needed
only a pen and a new tablet, signifying practice and a mind not
infected by depraved opinions.

This advice I think must also be followed in learning from Paul.
For the Scriptures, as they are pure in themselves, love to be poured
into pure minds. But you properly seek from Paul, as I said before,
Christ's grace, that is, the Spirit of virtues, whence he comes and
what he accomplishes in the minds of mortals. You will profit from
practice and frequent meditation when there is any ignorance, and
since you spend so much labor on inferior disciplines, you will do
well to cease from these when the matter of salvation is concerned.

I have summed up Pauline doctrine with fewer words, to be sure,
than such a weighty matter demands, but I had to conform to time;
otherwise it was my wish to follow this argument further. Meanwhile, as it is appropriate to regard nothing superior to a knowledge of Christ, it is fitting to strive in every possible manner that
you may understand as correctly as possible the grace of Christ.
Indeed, to know Christ is not thoroughly to examine the modes of
eternal generation or of the marvelous incarnation, but to know
the gracious acts by which he has opened up the way of salvation
to the whole wide world; it is to know why strictly speaking he came
to earth, what can be gained from him, of which things the flesh
which he assumed is a pledge, or the cross, on which he met his
death doubtlessly for our sake. This pursuit, finally, is both salutary
and one worthy of a Christian mind, and this is the philosophy
which Paul teaches. It is the grace of Christ, which all recent
theology treats with neglect but which Paul most fully follows.

Let others discourse about the stations of the winds, about the
forms of things, about motions, about thunderbolts; but Paul discusses the only things in which true and absolute happiness clearly
consists. To this are added innumerable topics unheard of by the
philosophers, such as: What can laws do in the attainment of virtue;
whence it is propagated; to what degree that force by which we
are carried headlong into vices, rages in human minds. These things
he brings in that the understanding of mortals may rule over the
passions. As he does this, it cannot be said with what great skill
he paints the portrait of man with his colors. Indeed, in this one area
the doctrine of Paul is most pleasing to me.

Very many love philosophy dearly because it paints the picture of man before his very eyes. And some of the ancients judged that they themselves knew the fruit and summit of philosophy. But how much more happily is this set forth by Paul, in whom it is possible to discern as in a mirror whatever is located within the deep recesses of man! You will in no place behold more absolutely the very nature of vices, in no place more exactly the strength and sources of virtue.

After we have in some degree learned from Paul, philosophy seems to us to spread certain shadows over the eyes of men, and in its estimate of man's nature, which it makes almost in the very beginning, and in discerning the definitions of vices and virtues, it seems to squeak, to be under hallucinations, and to be blind.

The common herd of theologians regard as crass and idiotic what Paul has set forth and think that these things can be learned in passing, as in successive study hours, while immersing their entire souls in their own rhapsodies. These, to be sure, are worthy fellows, who have this opinion, not to make any harsher remark of this kind, and they do not understand even two verses of Paul!

Now with reference to what pertains to the constitution of civil matters and to the errors of conscience, no man judges more considerately or prudently or with more fairness than Paul. And in keeping with him, it was fitting to regulate the laws of states and to seek formulas for the judgment of moral lapses. Many topics and figures of Scripture are added, which he has everywhere illustrated. Therefore let him incite you first with a care for your salvation, because outside of the doctrine of Paul, Christ, in whom is embodied the very sum and substance of salvation, cannot be known with exactitude.

Then there is a knowledge of many things which it is both pleasant and useful to know. If you want a succinct system of theological matters, if it is your interest to know what are the roots of vices and virtues, what their fruits, what habits are worthy of a Christian mind, what your obligation is to princes, to bishops, to the people, to yourself, to human and to divine laws, then no man teaches these things with more accuracy, no man more suitably than does Paul.

In the case of human literature, in the case of philosophy, it is a pleasure to unroll all the papyri of all the authors. In Scripture it would not help to be without the short commentaries of Paul, to which so many considerations call us. You want to console your mind and to meditate upon your Christ: Nowhere is he more aptly set forth. You want to be comforted: His speech is full of charms, pure, vigorous, lofty, elegant, clear. You desire to be exercised mentally: Here you have an argument which you may compare with the philosophers. With it you may indict the theologians of our age, who attribute to man absolute virtue apart from the power of Christ. It seems to me they owe this to their contempt for this one man Paul.

You have many other deep mysteries also concerning which you may speak. In such a type of exercise of your minds, with how much greater fruitfulness you will be occupied than in those cheap little debates of the schools into which so many superfluous and frivolous things, even many seeds of hatred, fall. It is pious to be occupied with the Scriptures, even a pleasant thing to be occupied with Pauline studies, where so many things are discussed with a certain marvelous charm.

And I want these things recommended to you as a model for every first-rate man. None of the ancients failed to give Paul the highest praise. Peter, if the title of that epistle does not deceive me, in an epistle that has certainly been received, diligently commends to Christians the letters of Paul. By common consent the church calls Paul the teacher of the Gentiles. In expounding him, Origen, Jerome, Chrysostom, Augustine, as well as many others labored with perspiration. Subsequently, when Christianity waned, he was for some time almost disregarded, but now in our times he is blossoming forth again for all active, first-rate scholars. Let their studies put the spur to you also, since that must be the best which is approved by the best men with such an overwhelming consensus. In the meantime, let us give thanks unto God who reveals Christ to us by the letters of Paul, and let us pray that God in his kindness may impart to us also the same spirit of knowing Christ which he bestowed on Paul.

LETTER TO THEOLOGIAN DOCTOR JOHN HESS OF NUREMBERG

Greetings from Philip Melanchthon

You see, my dear Hess, how certain critics right now are removing from the rank of Christian doctrines those very principles which we discussed at Wittenberg and which you, in accordance with the candor of your mind, so highly approved. It is particularly the statement about transubstantiation which I do not think I can number among the articles of faith. For Christian letters in our times are in such a condition that no man dares to call anything devout except what the schools profess has been commonly accepted. Hardly any other error has been more pernicious than this. For beyond question we see how it has come about that more concern is had for what the schools accept than for what Christ himself teaches.

To be sure, as for myself, being unwilling by strife to profane Christian letters, which constitute the only pledge of peace on earth, nothing would have taken precedence over my support of the schools, if the schools themselves were not in opposition to Christ in so many ways. Therefore it seemed best to submit to you in a few words the nature of my view so that you might have at hand something which you can reply to friends in my name.

Nor am I doing this to satisfy my critics, for these I know to be too captious to be placated by any plan whatsoever. With these few words I hope that I shall have satisfied you, a man both learned in purely Christian letters and a person of uncommon judgment in sacred matters. But first I remind you that I have proposed several statements to the schools for discussion. Concerning these it was my purpose to hear what all the best and most learned men thought. Badly diseased bodies once were exposed at public crossroads to be seen by all citizens so that if anyone had discovered the nature of the disease or anyone knew a remedy, he might so indicate. What prevents us from doing the same thing with respect to letters? May it not be permissible, if you are in doubt about anything, to appeal to the judgment of others?

I have determined to ascertain just what the doctors think about my view. I did not casually approve it to be sure, and I would withdraw my opinion with equanimity, but only if someone else were to counsel something better. The schools are calling in doubt even the most certain things, and may I not dispute about uncertainties and about those things which for so many ages only the few have agreed upon?

The practice of the schools ought to be rejected if it is not possible to argue about doubtful matters, unless it is not permissible for the Saxon schools alone to do what has been allowed the Bohemian and the Cologne schools and all schools everywhere. And so indeed we have proposed that we should argue, but be prepared to retract if anyone should teach more correctly. But those critics, although they are teaching nothing, nevertheless do falsely accuse us and raise their characteristic plaintive cry: "Heresy!" No rather, a new heresy! But let us investigate the matter itself a little more accurately.

In the list of our principles there are specifically two, and from them as if from a fountain, a third one about transubstantiation and "*character indelibilis*" is derived.

1. With respect to what is Catholic, it is not necessary to believe in any other articles than the ones Scripture approves.

2. Then, too, the authority of Scripture is superior to the authority of councils.

3. On the basis of the first two, it follows that it is not a crime of heresy not to believe in transubstantiation, indelible character and the like.

The last principle could not be wrested from its position unless you had refuted the two former ones. Moreover, the principle was applicable not only to transubstantiation or indelible character but also to all the members of this class, for which ordinarily the title of divine right is alleged. Why, then, do they send forth their plantive cry in the case of the article about transubstantiation only? Especially so since, indeed, the commentaries on the sentences differ not only with respect to indelible character but also on transubstantiation. May I not be granted the same privilege as they, seeing that I approach the Scriptures with perhaps more learning than the whole crowd of them? And to reveal to you the wisdom of my argument, I saw that the authority of Scripture was being everywhere diminished by human decrees. Not only were things human compared with the divine but even seemed to be preferred. Articles of faith were said to be not only what had been decreed in the councils of the holy fathers or things which the pontiffs had sanctioned, but also whatever Thomas or Scotus argued. And in them not only were many uncertainties defended as certainties, but also things that were improperly called Christian were handed down as things pious.

Since with respect to things of this nature, human narratives became of so much value, a judgment about sacred matters was sought not from the Scriptures but from human traditions. Nor do they regard what the Gospels teach as of so much importance as what men prove from the Gospels. Christ teaches that we must not seek revenge. No man dared to approve this, but it was referred to the schools, where we heard that it was a counsel, not a command, that no man should take revenge. O impious and wicked word! Paul thinks that a Christian commits a wrong if he contends in litigation with another; it was impiety to accept this because in this matter neither the canons nor the schools of theologians approved Paul.

And Christ forbade the use of the scepter by pontiffs, but today it is a crime not to arm with two swords those whom they call pontiffs. Finally, to say it in a few words, I myself have heard from jurists that disputations were relegated to the theologians, otherwise judgment of theological matters was with those who profess the things pleasing to the church. No doubt with these as judges, sacred matters have been rightly deliberated!

Now, with this reasoning, Hess, how many persons do you think have been called away up to now from the Gospel and have become aware that sacred matters must be sought not from Christ but from the lying traditions of men? I beseech you, am I doing an unwise thing to commend the Scriptures to the studious, when I call them away from human traditions, when I point out that judgment of sacred matters should be sought from the Gospel and not from any ditches you please?

These considerations showed why I set forth an argument about human regulations. I began to oppose their common opinions, and the argument that was deduced from other writers through unbelievable labyrinths, I brought to conclusion with just two propositions: A Catholic must believe Scripture alone, and the authority of Scripture is greater than that of the councils.

Would that all of us might strive eagerly to explain in as few words as possible the scholastic trifles of this kind. How many chapters, how many laws, how many titles they smeared compactly on their papers, as those who discussed this matter previously turned everything upside down! Each one busied himself with his own little project. This one was concerned with pontifical majesty and that one with the right of councils. No more account was ever taken of Scripture, than of the writings of the inhabitants of the city of Megara.

Why do I say more? You yourself will be permitted to see how in a matter clear in itself they play the rhetorician ineptly, with scarcely any scruples. You will see also how they declare by the very nature of their disputation that they are doing this not that they may explain, but just to impede the minds of the studious with certain hair splittings. On the contrary, I drew together the sum of the matter in two lines. If there is any mistake in them, why do they not lovingly point it out?

I minimize the authority of human traditions, but in order that in this way I might commend more highly the authority of Scripture. There are some who think that a short way to theological matters is not the Scriptures but certain summas, as they call them. When they have learned from them what is commonly thought about some matter, they measure Scripture according to them as if they were a rule. Would it not have been advantageous for them to be called back into the right way, that they might observe, not what has been accepted, but what ought to be accepted? Or if I have accomplished less with others, it is certainly worth my labor to have liberated at least my own self from the common opinion. For up to now we do not see what has come forth through human repetitions through which so many Christian principles have been made obsolete. Wars, interest, legal claims, and other things of this nature are now approved, and I do not see how they agree with Christ. The reasons for the Sacraments which these have produced plainly reek of Jewish ceremonies. The grace of Christ is ignored. Plato writes that there was an Egyptian law that no new song should be added to the sacred hymns. How much less should we permit a doctrine of sacred things, divinely produced and with the Son of God himself as author, to be changed by the lying traditions of men.

And Christ everywhere impresses upon us, and the apostles, whose letters by divine grace have been propagated even to our times, everywhere warn that we must beware of the traditions of man. See how their authority has in no way affected those who ensnare the church with so many sanctions and who entangle the schools of theology with so many trifles and such nonsense.

I appeal to you, Hess, you who have sailed the unfortunate ocean of questions but who now, as if saved from shipwreck, do enjoy securely the sweet delicacies of Scripture, what do you think about human traditions and the counterfeit schools? Do you not seem to be in another world? Does not now the spirit of Christ fashion you in a way different from that in which the schools once did? Do we not owe the destruction, so to speak, of Christianity and of divine Scripture to the doctrines of men? How much more to those who prefer anything whatever to returning us to evangelical studies?

The divine prophet Isaiah sings that it will come to pass that a sealed book of celestial mysteries is to be handed down to be read by those who have not learned letters, when he speaks about the teachers of human traditions. In this you may understand how aptly he accords with our times, in which the authority of sacred

Scripture has plainly become extinct when so much is attributed to human inventions. I am freeing my mind somewhat from human traditions, that if I have accomplished less in the case of others, I may surely commend to myself the pursuit of divine Scripture. There certainly was a time when I was frightened away from Scripture because I saw that what the Scriptures themselves teach was not so much opposed as that which has been received by most of the schools or the commentaries which obviously disagree with Scripture at many points. Now I am doing this that judgment in regard to all things sacred may be sought from Scripture alone and not from the doctrines of men. Let traditions have their own authority, but let the judgment of them be subject to Christ.

If I am wrong in this respect, surely I have never been more honorably wrong. But I am regarded as in error only by those who have taught nothing but human dreams, and to them the Scriptures do not mean exactly what they say but only what they themselves, infected with their depraved opinions, read into them.

Now what is the nature of the boast they make, that the interpretation of Scripture pertains to themselves alone? Just as if, indeed, Scripture has been so produced that it may not be understood except by our masters. On the contrary, the merciful Spirit of God has designed that Scripture be understood by all of the faithful with as little difficulty as possible. I beg you, let us not permit divine Scripture to become Egyptian hieroglyphs. The Son of God took upon himself flesh in order that he might not be unknown. And how much more has he willed to be known through the Scriptures which, as a sort of image of himself, he has left to us for a perpetual possession!

In view of the fact that this interpretation of Scripture of which they boast was born within the last four hundred years, I ask you, Before that time to whom did this interpretation belong? Certainly to all Christians in general, since the theological confession was not yet prepared for the stage, for the theater, or for party factions, but was the same for all Christians. As many of us as have been washed with the blood of Christ do profess him. What meanness is it to keep some of that number from Christ's doctrine? Therefore the investigation of holy Scripture should be permitted us also. Whatever we are, we certainly seem worthy to be called Christians, to whom those lofty teachers of ours should entrust this pursuit. Our Christ always zealously commands that his doctrine be promulgated with greatest faith and care. He condemns with words horrible to relate those who will not be hearers of his teaching. What reason is there that does not incite us to the Gospel?

Nor indeed has he willed human traditions to be propagated, but rather his own doctrine. What wrong is there if everywhere in some respect we call our minds away from the lying repetition of men? With this purpose, Hess, I proposed principles for dispute in order to urge that no man should seek a judgment about sacred matters from any other source except holy Scripture. Many are unrolling the regulations of the pontiffs; many, the summas; and many the skillful arguments of the theologians to seek the form of Christianity from these sources. In the midst of such a variety of interpretations, which we owe to those jesting theologasters alone, they do not think it is safe to trust in the Scriptures. They attribute so much to the fabrications of men that they estimate even holy Scripture according to them, as if they were a rule. In order to free myself from this error I take the position that it does not matter if anyone does not believe anything except what Scripture teaches. Accordingly we give primacy to holy Scripture, and we think that from it the judgment of all ecclesiastical matters must be sought. This is in accord with the testimony of Paul, who said when writing to Timothy: "Hold fast the pattern of sound words which thou hast heard from me." He commands that holy Scripture serve as an exemplar and archetype, and this he points out in many places.

But the authority of councils is so dependent upon Scripture that it is not permissible to decree anything contrary to them. For thus Paul writes to the Galatians: "If anyone shall have preached unto you other than what you have received, let him be accursed." Then, unless what has been decreed can be considered according to Scripture as certain, and unless it is something about which there must be no ambiguity, I do not accept it. That is wrong which has been decreed contrary to Scripture. That is ambiguous which Scripture has not fortified. For example, sin is that which is done against the Law, but it is ambiguous when one says that sin is that which is done outside the Law.

Those who attribute most unto the councils say that those whom the Holy Spirit has called in assembly cannot err in a matter of faith. Now, from what source will it be certain that these have been called together by the Holy Spirit, unless they decide what has for a certainty been produced by the Holy Spirit, and that, too, what Scripture approves—unless Paul in vain wanted Timothy to consider the source whence he had learned those things which he knew.

We know that what has been set forth in the Canonical Books is the doctrine of the Holy Spirit. We do not know that what is decided by the councils is the doctrine of the Holy Spirit unless it agrees with Scripture. It seems indeed that Christ indicates that a tree is to be judged by its fruits, especially since it is not agreed how far the Holy Spirit imparts himself to the councils, since it has been discovered that they so often have erred. The Apostle Paul writes about Christian doctrine to the Corinthians as follows: "No other foundation can be laid except that which has been laid, and if a man built upon it gold, silver, precious stones, wood, hay, stubble, the day of the Lord shall declare it." By this statement he means that if anything should be added to canonical doctrine, which is the foundation of Christianity, it must be left in the realm of ambiguities because, to be sure, the day of the Lord shall some day disclose it. The Spirit and prophecies are not to be condemned, but approved, as is written in Thessalonians.

Truly, is not the indicator or the Lydian stone according to which prophecies can be examined, Scripture itself? The commonly accepted statement that councils cannot err in matters of faith, I think, is spoken not a little too freely; surely it is beyond the authority of Scripture, although this very thing is being softened by some by a frivolous lie through the Graces. They are now saying that a council cannot err, but if it should err, it is not a council but a place for deliberation, and who is there that does not understand what this means? If either councils or what they call places for deliberation can err, surely there is need of Scripture as a judge either to confirm or to reject what has been decreed. Otherwise in what manner might we know whether it has been a council or a place for deliberation, in which that which by chance is called into question has been defined?

In his work *Against the Donatists* Augustine says: "Canonical Scripture of the Old and New Testaments by all of the later letters of the bishops is set forth in such a manner that it cannot be doubted and disputed whether that is true or right which has been decided was written in it." And a little later he says: "Councils which are held in individual regions or provinces yield to the authority of plenary councils which are held according to the whole Christian world without any ambiguities, and these plenary councils often, though prior, are themselves corrected by later councils."

You can see just what Augustine attributes to Scripture and what to councils, for he confesses that the latter can err, but he thinks it is wrong to doubt Scripture. Just recently audacity has proceeded even to the point where they denied that even a pontiff erred. In the times of Sergius there are said to have been some who were of the opinion that the Pontifex Maximus could neither err nor be damned. This is inconsistent not only with Scripture, but also with the common sense of mankind. And in the pontifical laws, not only the regulations of the councils, but also the canons of the pontiffs are compared with evangelical doctrine. For thus says Leo in more than tragic words: "For this cause the more clearly and with a loud voice I do not fear to proclaim that those things which we have affirmed, such as the statutes of the holy fathers, which are called canons, every man, be he bishop, cleric, or layman, is obligated to accept without indifference. Nor is he allowed to retain or to believe usefully and efficaciously for his own purpose either the Catholic or Apostolic faith or the four holy Gospels."

Who can bear such impudence? Well-ordered states measure their laws by natural equity. May not the church bring her principles into conformity with Scripture? If councils cannot err in a matter of faith, it does not make any difference whether the learned or the unlearned are called together in the synods. But if it does matter, what would hinder us from denying that synods can err? Does not the pontiff who thinks that it is wrong for the Roman See to be judged by a council call the authority of that council in question? In arguments about morals and in the settlement of litigations have not some rather memorable synods often erred, and some, too, even in matters of faith?

Wherefore, since by experience it has been discovered that councils can err, and since it has not yet been proved they cannot, why should I call the mere opinions of men articles of faith? I ask, now, Hess, apply your mind to this and contemplate the issue itself more fully. Scripture, which is, to use Paul's words, the exemplar and substance of faith, has been divinely produced; it is not right for the council to decide anything contrary to it. Nor is it sufficiently agreed that synods cannot err. If anything has been decreed in them that cannot be brought into conformity with Scripture, will you suffer it to be called an article of faith? To be sure, I wonder who were the authors that first spread abroad the notion that councils cannot err? The outstanding synods of the ancients decreed nothing, as far as I know, without the approval of Scripture.

Today transubstantiation has been decreed. The primacy of the

Roman pontiff has also been decreed, and this I number among probable opinions until I am thoroughly convinced by the Scriptures. Also at the Leipzig disputation the condemned articles of Constance were vaunted, and Eck did not attack Luther with any other more plausible argument. But it is proper for these to have only as much authority as Scripture allows. For that matter, I by no means unwillingly embrace the doctrine of transubstantiation, but I would not rashly number it among the articles of faith. That the true body of Christ is eaten is an article of faith, whatever the manner in which the sacred body takes on the form of bread. Accordingly, the proposition I have disputed about transubstantiation I shall not suffer to be called heretical until it becomes an article of faith that councils cannot err, that things Catholic which cannot be approved by the judgment of Scripture must be considered articles of faith, and that the authority of councils is equal to that of Scripture.

On the other hand, I know with what extreme freedom the schools shout, "Heresy!" It is heresy to speak otherwise than the canons of the transferring of the Roman Empire. For example, it is heresy to call the splendor *(species)* of Marcus Cicero beauty *(forma)*. It is heresy not to attribute both swords to the pontiff. It is heresy to think otherwise about the number of Sacraments than what Lombard writes. It is heresy to gainsay the bulls about indulgences. Today so much is permitted to some, that they approve or condemn anything they please in accord with their own desire. I have set before you in a few words the purpose and the nature of my position. I should not like you to think that I have taken this stand so tenaciously that I would not yield if anyone should advise more accurately. The public gymnasia of the schools permit many things to be disputed for the sake of experience, and in this pursuit let something be granted to us also.

Then, too, the chapters of my argument are now being contested by many writers, lest anyone think that this case is mine only. But would that Eck would produce something more certain in this matter, for he is so displeased by my opinions. It is agreed that there is no place for irritation in these affairs; let the case be pondered and let the propositions be compared with judgment and a certain care.

I do not want to deprive you of your own most delightful studies by reading ours any longer. If it seems good, I shall carry on at another time. In the meantime, while you were absent, three little books by Eck have been published against us. They so definitely convey Eck that even without a title, they can be attributed to the author. It does not appear that he retaliates calumnies with calumnies against Doctor Martin; therefore no response has been made up to now.

This little declamation on Paul delivered, in accordance with the custom of our Academy on Paul's festive day, I am sending to you. The difficulty of the argument warned me not to publish it, for I have treated the topic in a manner not very plausible, and in its interpretation I do not satisfy even my own mind. But I have followed the wish of my friends who bade me publish the work. If there is anything wrong in this, I will repair the damage in a short while, I hope, by treating the same matter more fully. You will give it to my friends to read, if their ears can endure it.

All of us here are anxious about you and wonder why, in the meantime, you have written no letter to us. To be sure, I am almost persuaded that what the poets have imagined about Lotus is true, since you appear to be so forgetful of the friends whom you left here. Whether I should charge this up to the joys of your Silesia or to the friends whom you are enjoying there, I do not know. Surely it was fitting that our argument also be considered. All of your friends greet you, especially Doctor Dominicus Schleupner, Johannes Appel, Ulrich Pindar, and Hermann Tuelich. A fond farewell, my Hess.

February 1520.

While Luther was engaged in his powerful literary activity in 1520, Melanchthon had already taken up his position at the university in Wittenberg and was beginning to bring Luther's position out into academic circles, as can be seen from the theses which he debated in 1520. In these Melanchthon drew a sharp distinction between theology and philosophy, and especially did he oppose the Catholic interpretation of the mass as a sacrifice. Luther was very much impressed with these writings and said as much in a letter which he wrote to John Voigt: "I send you also the theses of Melanchthon which are to be debated today; although remarkable, they are true."

CHAPTER FOUR

CIRCULAR THEMES

1520

1. The beginning of justification is through faith.

2. Love is a work of faith.

3. The distinction between "faith formed" and "faith unformed" is a false one.

4. For unformed faith, as they call it, is not faith, but false opinion.

5. For love necessarily follows faith.

6. Faith and love are the works of God, not of human nature.

7. Since Christianity is rest and absolute freedom,

8. It follows that satisfaction is not a part of repentance.

9. It likewise follows that in Christianity there is no outward sacrifice.

10. Therefore the mass is not a sacrifice.

11. Nor is the mass a work of such a nature that its fruit can be transferred to another.

12. Just as there is no efficacy in baptism for anyone except him who is washed, neither is there any efficacy in the mass for anyone but him who eats.

13. For just as baptism, so also is the mass a sacramental sign by which God witnesses that the remission of sins has been granted.

14. Since the whole of our justification is faith, no work can be called meritorious.

15. Therefore all works of mankind are truly sins.

16. Since the keys have been given to all Christians alike, the primacy of Peter by divine right cannot be asserted.

17. The form of happiness fashioned by Aristotle not only does not agree with Christian doctrine, but does not even agree with the common judgment of mankind.

18. Therefore it was better to seek the plan of happiness and similar passages in the Scriptures, and therefore in the very sources, rather than in the ignorant nonsense of an empty-headed sophist.

In his first disputations Melanchthon had already emphasized a keen conception of the dogma of transubstantiation and the mass, and Luther had given a thorough treatment of the same theological loci. Here in a most succinct manner Melanchthon brings together in one place the very essence of his thinking on these important and controversial issues of the early years of the Reformation. O. Glemen, a textual authority on the works of Melanchthon, places this work in the first half of November, 1521. In the "Supplementa" these theses are contained in Volume VI. A German translation appeared in 1525 under the title "Von der Messe, Propositiones." The following translation is made from the Latin text.

CHAPTER FIVE

PROPOSITIONS ON THE MASS
1521

1. The Gospel transmits three things: the doctrine of faith, the doctrine of works, and the signs of promises or of the word of faith.

2. Faith is righteousness.

3. Works are the fruits of righteousness.

4. Signs are neither righteousness nor the fruit of righteousness.

5. Moreover, they are neither good works nor sacrifices that are offered to secure the remission of sins.

6. But they are the means by which we may be both reminded and assured of the word of faith.

7. There are two signs of the New Testament, that is, of grace promised: baptism and participation in the table of the Lord.

8. Signs are handed down for the purpose of reminding and assuring our heart of the will of God.

9. The use of signs is of the nature of putting a seal on letters.

10. To behold a painted cross is not a good work, but only a sign reminding us of Christ's death.

11. To behold the sun is not a good work, but only a sign reminding us of the Gospel or of Christ.

12. So participation in the table of the Lord is not a good work, but a sign reminding us of grace given to us through Christ.

13. But participation in the table of the Lord is different from looking at a painted cross or the sun, in this respect that the sun

and the painted cross are not signs instituted by God, by which it is definitely signified that grace has been given to me.

14. Signs that are devised by men only remind, but the signs instituted by God, in addition to the fact that they remind, also assure the heart of the will of God.

15. It is not for this reason that I approve of images, but for the sake of an example this is said about images.

16. In this manner men think within themselves: "I would indeed freely believe in God if he should talk to me as he did to the fathers, and if he would likewise show me signs of his good favor just as he showed them to the fathers. When has he spoken to me directly as he did to Abraham, 'I will be thy protector,' or when has he showed me some such sign as he did to him when he supplied a ram in the place of his son who was to be offered as a sacrifice?"

17. In order to mitigate this distrust in the human heart, signs have been added to the Word, as it appears in all the stories of Scripture.

18. Gideon had many signs from which he could conclude that the Lord would not forsake his people, who were about to wage war in Palestine. But Gideon was in doubt whether God wished the war to be waged by him.

19. Therefore he demanded a sure sign from God by which he would know for a certainty that the people were to be preserved by his hands and under his leadership.

20. In like manner there are many signs of grace for Christians, beyond question all of the miracles of Christ, but they have not been instituted for the purpose of signifying that grace pertains to us.

21. Therefore there is this one and only use of the mass, namely, to strengthen faith in the heart.

22. And how necessary for the conscience and how pleasant this use of a sign actually is, the spiritual easily understand.

23. For what more joyful thing can happen to the conscience than to receive a sure sign of the will of God?

24. Unless the conscience is assured of the will of God, it is impossible for it to subsist.

25. Just as, for instance, the sight of a painted cross does not justify the beholder,

26. Just as acceptance of the sign of the fleece does not justify Gideon,

27. In the same manner the mass does not justify anyone.

28. Just as beholding a painted cross is not a work of such a nature as to make satisfaction either for our own sins, or for the sins of others,

29. And just as Gideon's acceptance of the sign of the fleece was not of such a nature as to make satisfaction for his own sins thereby,

30. So the mass is no sacrifice.

31. There is only one sacrifice, only one satisfaction. That is Christ. Beyond him there is none other.

32. The fleece signified success granted by God to Gideon.

33. In like manner participation in the table signifies the grace given to us in the Gospel.

34. Gideon offered up nothing in the fact that he accepted the fleece as a sign.

35. So we offer up nothing when we participate in the table of the Lord.

36. Therefore bread cannot be offered up in behalf of others.

37. Christ is the only sacrifice for our sins, and besides him there is none other.

38. The mortification of our old nature in Christ is a sacrifice and an oblation.

39. Likewise the mass is not of such a nature that the more often it is repeated, the more it offers to God.

40. Just as each man is baptized for himself, so each man partakes at the table for himself.

41. He rightly partakes who uses it as a sign to confirm his faith.

42. He sins who partakes with the idea of offering up something unto God.

43. There is no further use of the mass except to remind one of grace promised, and to assure the heart of grace promised, and of the will of God.

44. Therefore without the Word masses are useless.

45. Indeed the Word is always incomparably greater than the sign.

46. One can be without the sign, but not without the Word.

47. Moreover, if the Word is lacking, how do you know what is being signified?

48. The abuse of the mass ought to be abolished by the magistrates.

49. It should be done in the same manner in which Hezekiah destroyed the bronze serpent, or just as Josiah demolished the high places.

50. The abuses are that the mass is celebrated for others, for money, by compulsion, and by those ignorant of the Word and of faith.

51. But the abuse is the more abominable when masses are celebrated by hypocrites for a satisfaction, for sin, for a good work, and for a sacrifice.

52. The laity abuse the table of the Lord when by this work they believe that their sins are taken away, or that they make satisfaction for their sins.

53. For they ought to use it for a sign by which they might be admonished, first of the grace promised in the Gospel, and then as a means by which they might be assured of the benevolence of God toward them.

54. The mass is of no more value to the spectator than his beholding a picture.

55. It is to the advantage of the one who eats if by it he is admonished and assured.

56. Because of their trifling abuse of masses Paul writes that the Corinthians were wasted by a plague.

57. We ourselves, because of such abuse, undoubtedly are being punished by wars, by pestilence, and, what is most miserable, by blindness.

58. The more persistently one indulges in the abuse of masses, the more blindly one sins.

59. Especially is this so since the sin of public ignorance is the sin of each individual (Numbers 15).

60. Thus far participation in the table of the Lord has been treated, and now for some statements about prayers.

61. The prayers offered by priests in the mass are of no more efficacy than the prayer of a layman.

62. All of us are priests.

63. The priesthood is nothing more than the right to pray, or to importune God, or to make an offering to God.

64. Let Thomas and Scotus, who are the originators of this abuse of the mass, be anathema.

65. Let the bishops and the schools who do not oppose the impiety of the mass be anathema.

After the excommunication of Luther had been declared by the bull "Decet Romanum Pontificem" on January 2, 1521, the Sorbonne, which, after the Leipzig Disputation, was requested by Duke George of Saxony for a decision and reminded of the same by Frederick the Wise in March, 1521, was able to come to a decision more easily. So, on April 15, 1521, the Sorbonne faculty of religion published its "Determinatio theologorum Parisiensium super doctrina Lutheriana."[1] In it some one hundred and four principles of Luther were judged, mostly taken from his writing "De captivitate babylonica ecclesiae praeludium." No reference was made to the quarrel in the Dresden palace over the Leipzig disputation and especially over Luther's judgment about the papacy.

In June, 1521, Spalatin sent Melanchthon a draft of this writing, and the latter answered that he had received the same and had made a reprint of it in Wittenberg. The exact time of this is difficult to determine. However, Melanchthon wrote about it to Spalatin on June 14, 1521.[2] The work was published in October 1521. In his reply Melanchthon treated the Sorbonne without any forbearance. He placed the principle of Scripture over against the principle of tradition and established the contention that Luther's views agreed with those of the ancient church. At the same time he was in clear contradiction to Aristotle.

Luther was highly pleased with Melanchthon's Apology. On July 13, 1521, he wrote him about it.[3] The complete translation has been given again in W. A. 8, 267-312. Melanchthon's Apology there bears the title: "Widder das wuetende urteyl der Pariser Theologisten. Schutzred Phil. Melanchthon fuer Doctor Mart. Luther."

CHAPTER SIX

LUTHER AND THE
PARIS THEOLOGIANS
1521

See, Christian reader, what monstrous theologians Europe spawns, for last year the Sophists at Cologne and Louvain condemned the Gospel by setting forth bare statements which were confirmed neither by valid reasons nor by Scripture. The madness of these has been exceeded by the Parisians who have condemned Luther, whoever finally they are (for they cannot bring me to believe that this affair was done by the unanimous vote of the theological order).

In addition to the fact that in the former instance comparatively few things were condemned, how much more harshly and severely is Luther treated by the Parisians. In the first place, a bloody letter has been ascribed to him, and then there have been added wicked and atrocious annotations upon individual opinions of Luther. Many of his views have been distorted even in a sinister fashion. And from this source it can also be deduced what spirit and what madness move the authors of the decree, since the Spirit of God operates honestly. In general, the book is of such a nature that it would not be easy for any man to believe that it could have been written in Paris, since indeed it is commonly believed that in that school, as in some sort of fortress, the Scriptures hold sway. Nor can it be denied that from that place in time past some very weighty men have come forth, especially in the last century that great Gerson, a man full of the Christian spirit as it appears. "But," according to the proverb, "there was a time long ago when the Milesians were strong."

But if now those distinguished men were to come to life, do you think that they would recognize these judges, whoever they are, as their degenerate posterity? By no means! But they would deplore both the lot of the school and of the entire Christian state in which they would see sophists holding sway instead of theologians, and slanderers instead of Christian teachers. And they would recognize this to be a time such as the church in Jeremiah's age deplored with these words: "The Lord has taken away from the midst of me all of my distinguished men and has called against me time to consume mine elect."

When I consider the matter more properly, however, it seems that this is not the first time they have been wrong in Paris. For some time now they have been talking trifles when ecclesiastical doctrine, vitiated by human arguments, began to philosophize. For it is agreed that in Paris was born that profane scholasticism which they wish to be called theology. And when this has been admitted, there is no salvation left for the church. The Gospel has been obscured, faith rendered extinct, the doctrine of works received, and instead of being a Christian people, we are a people not even of the Law, but of the morals of Aristotle. And out of Christianity, contrary to every intent of the Spirit, there has been made a certain philosophical plan of living.

Would that it might moisten your spiritual eyes to discern how much damage has been done to the church by that scholasticism of yours, both born and perfected among you, which the rest of Europe's schools have received from you as from your very hands! It has become positively reasonable that the earth is filled with idols. And your articles assuredly testify how persistently you have philosophized all of the way from the very origin of scholasticism up to now. And in those articles how few there are which relate to piety. At what do such things aim? "I [he] runs" (*ego currit*) is an absurd mode of speaking and there is a difference, I know not what, between these two modes of speaking: "of whatsoever man's ass runs" and "the ass of whatsoever man's runs." The aim is clear: dogmas that are worthy of a Christian school!

And now that it has been openly decreed that philosophical disciplines are necessary for piety, do we not see just what article has proceeded from what spirit? To be sure, from that spirit that has wished for the Gospel to be obscured by human disciplines. It is indeed clear how the attempt has succeeded in this respect. For what school has taught purely the holy Scriptures? Although the school of Paris indeed for so many years up to the present has pursued philosophy, in these times she has ceased to philosophize and only talks nonsense about their trifling *Logicalia*.

For who is more trifling than John Versor, Peter Tartaretus, and other writers of such a quality as those whom Paris has produced in this century in almost innumerable amounts? I have seen John Major's Commentaries (I do not judge the man's character) on the Sentences of Lombard. He is a man who they say is predominant in Paris among the theologians! What a wagon load of nonsense! How many pages does he use to dispute about whether a horse is required for riding, whether the sea was made salty by God! But I shall pass over the many impious things which he has written about free will, for on that topic he differs not only from Scripture but also equally from all the Scholastics. And since the Parisians are of such a kind, there is no reason for you to wonder, my reader, why they are not so favorable to Luther. Formerly they were no more favorable to their own Gerson, a man great in all respects, when the schools of Paris were saner.

Now, just what would happen when all things are full of scholastic dross? Moreover, I know full well that there are some there also to whom Luther is not pleasing, but it is accustomed so to happen, not only in sacred but also in civil matters, especially indeed in sacred matters, both that the good ones are too few and that they have most power who ought to have least. This is what Homer also saw, though blind, when he said: "The worse conquer." For who does not know, in the case of Capnio (Reuchlin), through what ghosts the affair was handled?

When the faculty was said to have made the decree—seven in all, if I mistake not, and among them some monks, had assembled, who, as they themselves said, were representing the faculty. What if the same thing has happened here? Although it is not important who made the decree, we must consider what the decree is.

The apostle orders that the Gospel must not be given up to those who are corrupting it, not even if they are angels. Shall we give it up to those insipid ones and to our thoroughly stupid masters, who have not even learned correctly their own little *Logicalia?* Neither powers nor principalities wrenched the apostle from the Gospel. Should these ghosts of men separate us from it? For what are they but ghosts? Let the name of our masters have strength, let the name of the Parisians have strength, but only in their own schools. In the Christian state let nothing have strength besides the voice of Christ, which, if any man does not hear, he is none of Christ's.

It was not of any consequence to answer wholly, since nothing is being opposed to Luther except some bare propositions. For Luther has so strongly fortified his positions on every side with Scripture (especially in that little book which he inscribed *Declaration of the Articles Condemned by Leo X*) that they cannot be judged wicked except by the wicked. Nevertheless, I should like to point out in a few words one or two topics from which you can more freely evaluate the rest and judge the whole decree.

In the first place, if the letter which they have prefixed to the decree is not that of some hired rhetorician, then that theologian who did write the letter, which contains nothing but some ravings of a woman, is exceedingly foolish. For what, I ask you, are these statements like? "He alone pretends to be wise, he hates us, he is Manichaeus, he is Montanus, he is crazy. Let him be coerced by fire and flame because his wrath has not allowed him to speak consistently."

Moreover, in this particular also the people will greatly wish for common sense in that false faculty which says that Luther must be destroyed by fire rather than conquered by reason. At this point, who would not laugh at this feminine and plainly monkish impotence? And with evidence I should be permitted to warn the admirable Lord Dean: "Forbear, Lord Dean, you are already enraged. Do you not know what the poet said, 'Fury and rage cast down the mind'?" Never have those at Cologne or Louvain talked trifles so freely, so that I almost believe that certain of the ancients were not speaking altogether rashly when they said that the Gauls were without understanding.

They accuse Luther of heresy, not because he disagrees with Scripture, but with the universities, the holy fathers, and the councils. And then they call the opinions of the universities, of the holy fathers, and of the councils the primary principles of faith. At this point I could contend with you about your decree also, if the matter is obscure. But what is clearer than the fact that neither the universities, nor the holy fathers, nor the councils can establish articles of faith, since it can happen that not only the universities err, but the holy fathers and the councils likewise? If you do not believe me in this respect, then believe your own Ockham at least.

Why, therefore, do you call the opinions of men principles of faith? Who is ignorant of Paul's statement, "No other foundation can be laid save that which has been laid"? For he is speaking of doctrine. What new articles of faith will our Parisian masters add except perhaps their own stinking articles, concocted in their own cook-shops? Now since there are no articles of faith except those which have been prescribed by sacred Scripture, why is it wicked for us to differ either with the councils or the universities, provided we do not differ with Scripture? But Luther does not differ with Scripture even according to your judgment. Why then is he accused of impiety? He disagrees with the interpretation of Scripture which up to this time has been received through the fathers, the councils, and the schools. This is, as I see it, the sum of the controversy. And here I ask you, my masters, has Scripture come forth in such a manner that its certain meaning can be established without the interpretation of the councils, the fathers, and of the schools, or not? If you will deny that the meaning of Scripture by itself is certain without glosses, I do not see why it was necessary that Scripture be produced if the Holy Spirit was unwilling to establish with certainty what he wants us to think. Or why do the apostles invite us at all to the study of Scripture, if its meaning is uncertain? What of the fact that to the extent to which the fathers want us to believe them, to that same extent they fortified their positions by the evidences of Scripture? What of the fact that even the ancient councils made no decree without the Scripture? It is by this plan that we discern the true and the false in the councils, because these councils evidently concur with Scripture while those differ from Scripture. Therefore, you will grant me that the meaning of Scripture is certain and clear, so that if any passage anywhere is rather obscure, Scripture itself explains itself.

Especially is this true with reference to those things which the Holy Spirit has willed to be known and believed. Moreover, he willed that the Law be known in no doubtful manner inasmuch as he has ordered it to be inscribed upon the doors of houses and to be engraved on the fringes of garments. Likewise he has willed that the Gospel be known, that is, the plan of righteousness bestowed through Christ. For since the Word of God should be a rock on which the soul rests itself, I ask you, what will one think of the Word if it is not certain what the meaning of the Spirit of God is?

Now, since the meaning of Scripture is certain through itself, it ought to be preferred, not only to the schools or the fathers, but also to the councils which have opposing judgments. As the apostle says in Galatians: "If an angel from heaven preaches another gospel than the one we have preached, let him be anathema." Therefore, let Luther be permitted to place the certain meaning of Scripture over against the councils, the fathers, and the schools.

What will you say here in reply, you Sophists? What glosses will you oppose to us at this point? What little *Logicalia?* What obligations will you devise? Either deny that the meaning of Scripture is sure or else permit Luther to place Scripture over against any persons whatsoever who think differently.

Nor shall we now grant to you that Luther is opposed either to the fathers or to the councils. And indeed, to speak first of the fathers, is not Luther's view on free will and grace the whole view of Augustine, if you rightly judge the matter? And besides, Luther follows him throughout in his commentary on Galatians. The commentaries of both are extant. If you compare them, you will observe an agreement between them on the sum of the matter.

Augustine's books against the Pelagians are extant, which he wrote when advanced in years. If you compare them with Luther's doctrines, you will see that they agree on the sum of the matter. Perhaps another somewhere has said something more subtly, and Luther (burst forth in the meantime, our masters) has said many things more diligently than Augustine. This does not make so much difference for the heart of the matter. Behold how in the primary topic as well as in that in which Luther especially reigns he has Augustine and a far from ordinary person voting with him. He has likewise as many witnesses for his view as voted with Augustine in that argument of his. Again, Cyprian supports him, for he faithfully quotes his interpretation of the Lord's Prayer. And those who wrote after Augustine also vote with Luther as well as the author of the book *On the Calling of the Gentiles,* a certain Maxentius among the Greeks, for it does not seem to belong to Ambrose. Moreover, we receive from Augustine's books those whom he himself wanted especially to be approved.

I am enumerating these things not because I think that it makes a great difference what the writers thought, whoever they finally are, when the meaning of Scripture is settled, but to satisfy those captious souls who think that Luther has changed everything, when he has done nothing else than to call us back to Scripture and also to the fathers who came the closest to the meaning of Scripture. But what do you do? Anything other than let the minds of Christians become great in the formalities of Scotus and in the connotations of Ockham rather than in Christ? You oppose the rising light of the Gospel (hear, you Sophists, who will not understand) as Moses was opposed by Jannes and Jambres, whose posterity is the family of Sorbonne, beyond doubt descendants from that Egyptian "Sorbonnity." Moreover, with what degree of trustworthiness at various times you have quoted passages from Augustine against Luther, I will advise you a little later on. And apart from the topic on free will and grace, it is a tradition by now that Luther does not want the Law to be distinguished into counsels and precepts. We owe this fabrication to scholastic theology alone. When it began to consider the divine Law according to the philosophy of Aristotle, it abrogated for the sake of lust whatever laws of God it wanted to annul.

For who of the ancient writers did not consider as necessary laws those things which have been decreed about not taking vengeance? Hilary says: "The Gospels cast out the pretense of avenging an injury." Augustine in his comment on the Sermon of the Lord on the Mount calls precepts what they call counsels and he argues in such a manner that it appears that the law about not taking revenge is necessary. Chrysostom is also of this view and is so far from permitting one to take revenge that he tenaciously demands no other law. His *Homily* is extant, and this, my masters, read again if it is permitted you through your little *Logicalia*.

We do not labor the point that the Law does not agree with the philosophy of Aristotle. For what is that to us, what that dirty man has contrived? We should not make Aristotle more than Christ, should we? But concerning this law I shall discuss many things in a little while. In many other places the same things can be shown, that Luther agrees with the ancients. But since from his view on free will and grace for the most part there can be deduced those things which Luther has written about contrition and satisfaction, what is the use of carrying on with many testimonies of the fathers, which are "nothing but a lamp at noonday."

Moreover, there are some things among the Lutherans which you would not easily discover in the writings of the fathers: the works Lutheranism has produced or such issues as the number of Sacraments, Confession, vows, and similar matters of our times. For reason in those times and the purer Christianity before today did not bear that there be fewer doubts than now. This present age had not yet had the tyrannical laws of the pontiffs nor our Parisian masters and therefore the articles of the Parisians which had so obscured the Gospel. Perchance that was the noonday of the Gospel, but now it is the evening. And together with our sins, our blindness also, the atrocious penalty of our sins has seized our minds and it has supplied human doctrines, that is, the theology of the Sorbonne, instead of the Gospel. Does not the Spirit of the Lord in the prophets everywhere threaten these times with punishment? And again, Paul said: "There will be those who depart from the faith and who corrupt the Gospel with the doctrines of man," and many such things. I do not understand what the apostle means by "those" unless he means the theologians of the Sorbonne.

You see, reader, that for the most part there is general agreement between Luther and the ancient theologians. How much more equitably, therefore, have we retorted to our Parisian masters that they are foolish who prescribe for us a theology which was never thought of by the most celebrated teachers of the church, not even in a dream. If it is impiety in any respect to gainsay the fathers, no man is more wicked than those Parisian disputers who, in the chief topics of theology, are, as it were, diametrically opposed to the fathers. A good portion of the fathers call sin and vice whatever is done without the Spirit of Christ. The Parisians not only do not call this sin, but they think that certain moral works (thus they speak) constitute merit of congruence. O blindness! A good portion of the fathers deny that the Law can be kept by man through his own powers; but these Parisians make a distinction.

Hear, reader, these Parisian blasphemies: the Law can be kept as far as the substance of the works is concerned; it cannot so far as the intention of the one who gives the Law, just as if indeed the lawgiver requires something else in addition to the substance of the work. Would, O Parisians, that the opportunity were given me to debate these matters face to face with you in your Sorbonne so that I might see whether such a crass, such a corrupt, and such a Sorbonnic falsehood would shame you! It is your theology, my masters, and not Luther's, that disagrees with the fathers. Those horrible doctrines of yours, that those who differ with the teachers of the church are wicked, pertain to you.

Now, indeed up to this point I have spoken about the doctors. Let us now look at the councils. In a word, what councils does Luther oppose? You want it to seem as if Luther's doctrine has been condemned by the councils of the ancients when you try to make him out to be a Montanus, a Manichaeus, an Ebion, or what not. Or at this point that author of the epistle, than whom there is none else at the Sorbonne who is more shameless and wicked, has evident-

ly wanted to play the rhetorician. But who is it that does not smell
out the reason why they have heaped up the names of ancient heretics upon Luther? To be sure, just to make the name of Luther to
become more odious. Then, too, how wickedly this has been done
even the moderately learned will easily comprehend. For in the
comparison of Luther with Montanus, who does not see how deceit-
fully this is done? Montanus wanted himself to be believed and
trusted in a certain spirit of his own. Luther in no way wishes himself to be believed, but only evident and clear Scripture. He in no
way boasts of his own spirit but of the Scriptures. How much more
nearly you resemble Montanus when you wish us to believe in the
spirit of men, of councils, of the fathers, and of the universities
more than in the Scriptures. On the contrary, I mean that you,
Parisian Sophists, are nothing but Montanuses who have published
this decree without Scripture and you boast that you trust in your
apostolic character as if it were agreed that the same Spirit is in
you that was in the apostles. But about this later.

I ask you, Christian reader, do you think that there is a Christian
spirit in that Sorbonne which is not at all ashamed to tell such lies?
For although it is plain to the Sorbonne itself that there is no agreement at all between Montanus and Luther, nevertheless it dares to
disgrace this very fine man with the name of Montanus. And besides, it has made him out to be an Ebion in a similarly deceitful
and reckless manner. Ebion threw out ceremonies and laws. Luther
does not throw them out but allows their use to be free, so that
anyone may accommodate himself to them in accordance with opportunity and the duty of charity, or may obey a rite or neglect it
without blame. For so Paul felt also, as he writes in the last chapter
of Galatians, when he places all ceremonies and rites on an equal
basis: "In Christ Jesus neither circumcision nor uncircumcision
availeth, but a new creature." And in 1 Corinthians 7, he writes,
"He who has been called in circumcision, let him not seek to be
uncircumcised." That is, if you have been called among those who
observe the Law, conform to their custom. "But whoever has been
called in uncircumcision, let him not be circumcised. Circumcision
is nothing and uncircumcision is nothing, but the fulfillment of the
laws of God, etc." I am of the opinion that it is quite clear just what
is the difference between the two views, and I also think it is plain
with what honesty they have distorted Luther's view over into the
heresy of Ebion.

It is the same kind of charge when they call Luther Manichaeus,

in the same way as the Pelagians accused Augustine, as he himself
confesses in the second chapter of the First Book against the Two
Epistles of the Pelagians, for so has the scribe, whoever he may be,
designated them. The insult will not shame Luther since he has it
in common with Augustine, than whom the Manichaean faction had
no stronger enemy. The writers of scholastic theology are Pelagians
—no, rather they are more vile than Pelagians. Therefore there is no
reason for us to wonder why you call Luther Manichaeus, you who
know nothing besides scholastic exercises which are doubly Pelagian.
Moreover, it is clear from the apology against the epistles of the
Pelagians that Augustine excuses the name of Manichaeus. And in
that place it seems that he discusses more aptly the bondage of the
will than when he debates with Felix Manichaeus. And if you
accept it, Augustine supports us also. But if the Parisian masters
are so blind that they really think that there is no difference between the opinions of Luther and those of Manichaeus, who, I ask,
is more blind than this sort of person? Again, if through malice
they attribute to him things which they know in no way relate to
him, what is more wicked?

But the Manichaean view is more far-reaching than should be
examined here, because it differs from Christian dogma in its whole
scheme of doctrine, if indeed we can trust Augustine, who is everywhere surveying the dogmas of Manichaeus. But the thing that does
relate to this particular cause is that Manichaeus denied freedom
of the human will in such a manner that he argued that it was not
a substance that should be renewed and, therefore, capable of
freedom. Luther denies freedom in such a way that he thinks that
it is a substance which, while it is renewed by the Spirit, nevertheless is liberated from its bondage.

From these remarks, reader, make your own conjecture about the
rest. For by this faithfulness these very same things and many
others which I have enumerated have been distorted upon Luther!
I return now to the point from which I digressed. It is clear that the
ancient councils have not condemned Luther's doctrine, seeing
indeed that it agrees with heretics in no respect whatever. Nevertheless, at this point it had to be considered how very great an
agreement there is between Luther and them, in what manner anything in the individual factions of heretics has been condemned,
for what heresy has been so deplored that has not been right in
some respect?

Now these things I am writing, not because I mean that the

authority in the early councils is such that if Luther opposes evident
Scripture to any council, Scripture must be abandoned. But I write
to warn the reader how much credibility ought to be placed in
those tragic words of the Parisian masters: Luther condemns all
of the councils and the holy fathers; he is Montanus; he is Ebion;
he is Manichaeus; he is Artotyrites—and other charges of this kind.

Moreover, within this time of the kingdom of the Roman antichrist there have been held several papal councils which Luther
has confessedly opposed, but with clear Scripture leading the
way. And besides, why should he not oppose them when in them
so many wicked things have been instituted against the Gospel?
That the keys of the church are common to all is denied by the
Council of Vienna. That the church is the whole assembly of the
predestined was denied by the Synod of Constance. The same council decreed that there are some good works apart from grace. These
views are certainly diametrically opposed to the Gospel. Therefore,
let Luther oppose those councils, under the leadership of Christ,
against whom those who made the decree were not the church of
Christ, but of antichrist. Did these Synods of Lyons and of Vienna
err in no way when they approved the epistles of the pontiffs?
Among these, who could bear the chapter *Ad Abolendam*, likewise
Venerabilem? Why is it, then, that you theologians of the Sorbonne
boast only of the Councils of Sorbonne? You cannot deny the fact
that nothing can be instituted contrary to Scripture, and that if any
decree is made contrary to it, it can be removed. Grant Luther,
therefore, the right to measure the decrees of the councils according to the Gospel. Grant him the right to prefer the Gospel, if
anything has been instituted contrary to it.

It is the right even for angels to yield to the Word of God. Let
the gates of hell also yield to it and let those manikins to whom we
owe the papal constitutions yield to it. It is not about universities
that we labor, for scholastic theology, if you please, has proved that
all the schools are heretical. At this point, cry out, my masters: "He
has blasphemed. He accuses the schools of heresy." Rightly so, if
they teach things that differ with the Gospel. And the scholasticism
of the Parisians does differ. It alone now reigns in almost all of
Europe's schools, and especially at Paris. Therefore there is no
reason, reader, for you to wonder why Luther is opposed to the
schools, which Micah calls the dwelling places of falsehood.

"But who would believe that so many err?" you say. They err as
many as teach something that differs from Scripture, as many as

approve that wicked scholasticism. But so many? Indeed! For truly
in Samaria among how many priests of Baal how few there were
of Elijah! Set before your eyes the entire history of both Judah and
Samaria, in which there is a prelude to the church, and see how
few prophets and how many idolaters! And in the last time, how
many Sadducees and Pharisees, that is, how many priests and monks
and scholastics you may find. There is nothing obscure, is there
about the saying of the Prophet Ezekiel: "Like mother, like daugh-
ter"? We have imitated, no rather, we have surpassed all of the
portents of the synagogue, so that even that can seem pious in
comparison with us, to use the prophet's word.

You understand, I believe, how much Luther agrees with the
fathers and the councils, although religion forbids him to agree with
the schools. Now consider how wise those Sorbonners are when
they call the fathers, the synods, and the schools the first principles
of faith. Nevertheless—unless I am seeing nothing at all—it does not
grieve them because there is some contradiction of the fathers and
the synods, but because scholasticism is treated too unworthily.
For scholasticism is that famous Helen for whom our masters are
fighting. Perchance you did not write thus in that clearly Sorbonnic
preface of yours: "We are our own masters and we teach scholastic
theology. We have nothing to do with Scripture and the Scriptures
have nothing to do with us. It is a struggle about our kingdom,
unless we have thrown out of the synagogue those who do not
receive scholasticism. All things must be moved and disturbed by us
lest scholasticism fall; and unless it is saved, we shall perish. Thus
let it be: although there is agreement between Luther and the
Scripture, the ancient fathers and the synods, let him perish, unless
he rejects them and adores us. We are the first principles of faith,
not Scripture. Nor indeed must we fight this man with reason,
especially when he denies the first principles, that is, the dreams
of our Sorbonne masters. Let him be flogged, let him perish because he denies the first principles."

It was madness to call the synods and the fathers the first principles of faith, since no other foundation can be laid than Scripture.
And it is insolent madness to prefer the falsehoods of the Sorbonnics to Scripture. Let not him who differs from Scripture be a
heretic, but let him be a heretic who differs from the French Sorbonners!

But away with their foolishness, for what consequence is there
in such a clear issue just to waste words? For what is clearer than

what I said before, that the views of the synods of the fathers and of the schools ought to yield to clear Scripture. But now I am following other aspects of the Sorbonnic epistle. Whom will he believe, they say, who refuses to have the faith of the Catholic Church or how will he be reckoned among the Catholics who does not hear the church, although it has been spoken from the very mouth of truth: "If he will not hear the church, let him be to you as a Gentile and a publican."

Moreover, I ask you, masters, what do you call the church? Is it that French Sorbonne? But how can that be the church which is foreign to the Word of Christ, since Christ testifies that his sheep know his voice? We call the church that which has been founded by the Word of God, which feeds on the Word, which is nourished, fostered, and ruled by the Word and, in short, that which compares all things according to the Gospel and judges all things according to the Gospel: "For he who is of God heareth God's words." Again, those who do not hear are not of God. And besides, since the church has been born of the divine Word, there is no doubt but that she must be nourished by the same.

Luther will recognize you as the church if you teach the Word of God, but he will not recognize you if you produce nothing besides your silly and nauseating articles. He listens to the church, but only that church which professes the Word of God. And he submits to the judgment of that church which demands nothing that is not according to the Word of God and which follows the judgment of holy Scripture and not the judgment of Sorbonnic dreams. For what sort of monstrosity will the church be if it changes in accordance with the falsehood of every Sorbonnic dreamer? What sort of chameleon, what polyp, rather what Proteus can be more changeable?

When Christ said: "If he will not hear the church, let him be to you as a Gentile or a publican," did he not intend that the guilty be accused before the church? Besides, he intended that the guilty be convicted through witnesses, that judgment be rendered according to a rule, the Gospel. You condemn Luther before you have accused and convicted him according to the Scriptures. Certain naked articles wholly without Scripture and without reasons are set forth, and in them Luther is not now being accused but is being condemned by you.

To dismiss other things, the Sorbonne alone is not the church, is it, that it excludes Luther from the communion of the devout? You should have accused him, not condemned him. You should have written down the testimonies of Scripture, not set forth naked articles; you should have entrusted him to the judgment of the church. Now you, after having changed the order both of divine and human law, are not accusing him or convicting him, but only condemning him and that too simply, because you are our Sorbonnic masters. Finally, let France be ashamed of the Sorbonne for being so insanely wicked.

But am I not foolish also to treat the Sorbonne so irreverently when it is producing new apostles at this time! For our masters say that they are following the example of the apostles when they set forth certain bare opinions without the authority of the Scriptures. But I would that they brought forth the apostles for our consideration not only in this one respect! Christ cites the authority of the Scriptures, wanted himself to be believed because of the support of Scripture. Paul voiced almost nothing but the words of another, that is to say, the words of the Old Testament Scriptures. And what are the sermons of the apostles but testimonies about Christ from the Old Testament? Shall we believe the Sorbonne alone, without the Scriptures?

Come forth from your Sorbonnic cave, our masters, into the light so that we may see whether such foolish men have any eyes or face. Doubtless the apostolic office was instituted to produce dogma without testimonies although not even Christ wanted himself to be believed without the Scriptures! Indeed we are comparing the work of the apostles with that of the Sorbonne! The question of the rites of the law was set forth as is recorded in the Book of Acts, Chapter 15. In that place when the divine Spirit had signified by various testimonies of Scripture and clear arguments and signs that the Gentiles were not to be burdened with Jewish ceremonies, a decree was made about liberty. At this point I ask you, masters, by what signs, by what evidences of Scripture were you forced to make a pronouncement about Luther? But it goes without saying that we shall not be so rash as to believe even in signs; Scripture alone we believe. In the next instance, they say they are chosen to bring the commands of the apostles with a living voice and to strengthen the faith of the churches. Whom do you send to the churches to set forth to them the reason of your view? Finally, they add an epistle in which they allege the witness of the Holy Spirit when they say: "It seemed good to the Holy Spirit and to us." What spirit do you allege?

Hear, you deaf vipers, what spirit do you allege to the world as a witness of your doctrine? The apostles alleged the Spirit of God and they were certainly assured through Scripture of the will of the divine Spirit. Presently even the churches were assured of the apostolic spirit. But what shall we think about your spirit? What if someone should say to you what that one said in Acts: "Jesus and Paul I know, but who are you"? What of the fact that the apostles, although they cited the testimony of the Spirit, did not write in such a manner as to think they gave satisfaction in such a case by a bare epistle, but added messengers to confirm the churches by a full message. The churches need this message and not dogmas. And Peter wishes Christians to be prepared to give a reason for their faith.

The whole world demands this of you also, our masters. Already before this it was clear in the schools what Paris was thinking. For your commentaries and your scholastic arguments are extant. Now the reason for that doctrine of yours is being sought. For those articles against Luther could have been gathered up from Gabriel or Scotus by some little boy in the middle of Germany. It is not so obscure what Paris teaches, but it is obscure why she teaches so. Luther demands the reason for your doctrine, not dogmas. For beyond question he would not condemn what he did not know. And would that you return to your mind and think about the greater things to be done by Luther rather than about those things which ought or can be entrusted either to the Parisian school or to Luther without the witness of Scripture. Those who favor Luther favor him in such a way because he has rejected human falsehoods, and they see that he teaches nothing but what the Scriptures themselves have produced. These same persons will believe you if they understand that you agree with Scripture, since they seek Christ both from Luther and from you.

You think that you possess the talent to sing a song like David's, for thus the prophet speaks, but you are singing only for yourselves and that which is within you. Luther sings his own song, that is, he proves his doctrine to the whole Christian world by the supports of Scripture. You hold that to Christians these Scriptural supports are nothing. "We are our own masters," you say, "we are Parisians, we are Sorbonnics, we are the parents of all diatribes." Vain are the names to which Germany now has almost become deaf. Wherefore I urge that if you want to atone for the reproach of wickedness, you set forth the reason for your judgment about Luther. Consult together with the Lutherans not about dogmas but about the arguments for your dogmas, unless you do not want to be regarded as Christians. Declare sometime by what spirit Luther has been condemned by the apostles of the Sorbonne. Not only is the Christian world now waiting for this, but it even demands by the right of Christian duty that you show in what respect and why you have condemned him.

And in order that I may finish up sometime, it seems good to show in one or two places just what unfamiliarity with sacred matters and what wickedness there are at the Sorbonne. For from these the rest can easily be estimated. Luther has written thus on free will: "Without grace, it cannot do anything but sin." The thing is well known and plain if you but consider Scripture. For thus speaks the Apostle Paul: "The mind of the flesh is enmity against God. For it is not subject to the law of God, neither indeed can be. Those who are in the flesh cannot please God." And John I: "Who have been born not of blood nor of the will of the flesh, nor of the will of man, but of God." And Augustine, following Scripture, deals the same way with the Pelagians, that is, the Sorbonne Sophists, not merely in one place.

In this matter those at the Sorbonne conceal Scripture and dispense with Augustine with a Sorbonnic falsehood, in which alone you will apprehend Sorbonnic blindness. And if it has ever been doubted in what kind of literature or arts Paris was engaged, it would now be made known in respect to this topic, in which it is clearly apparent that there is no one on that whole Sorbonne faculty who has come in contact with Augustine. What their ability is in Scripture itself can be easily estimated when they have not even seen Augustine, a common and well-known writer among theologians. O theologians! O Sorbonne! When Augustine in his dispute about grace says that free will cannot do good works without grace, they say that he is not talking about grace doing something pleasing. Blindness of blindnesses and blindness in all things!

Finally, what kind of grace does that illustrious man discuss? When so often he writes that Pelagius makes different uses of the word grace, he declares that he himself demands a grace that justifies or the Holy Spirit diffused into the hearts of those justified. Gifts of nature he plainly rejects, and he is ignorant of the special Sorbonnic aid. How, therefore, can it be that he is not speaking of justifying grace? And in order that we may evaluate the matter itself, I ask you, Sorbonnic Sorbonners, from what source have you secured the phrase, "grace doing that which is pleasing"? Is it not from the fact that it alone conciliates God? Since this is so, why do you imagine that something has been accepted without grace that does what is pleasing to God? Your words and your dogmas fight among themselves. You accept the phrase, "grace doing what is pleasing," but you do not accept the force of the phrase.

But let us see in what respect Augustine used the word grace. I could include his whole book on *The Spirit and the Letter*, since there is no page on which some mention is not made of grace. But these are his words in Chapter 4: "But when the Holy Spirit does not aid us by inspiring a good longing in place of an evil desire, that is, by diffusing love in our hearts, actually that law, 'Thou shalt not covet,' however good it may be, actually increases evil desire by forbidding it." Now what kind of grace is he here talking about when he plainly says that you cannot do anything without grace except sin? Does he not call grace the love of the Holy Spirit diffused in our hearts?

Now, you Sorbonners, what else do you call grace but love? Allow me to ask, not that you re-read Augustine, but that you simply look into him. For there is no page that does not clearly demonstrate your error. In the ninth chapter on grace he introduces the apostle, who says: "The righteousness of God through faith in Jesus Christ for all who believe." Can these words be twisted into the gratuitous gifts of nature or to special aid? O you rude and truly Sorbonnic masters of ours, who then will believe that you have either eyes or a mind or a brain when in such clear light you are so obscurely blind in everything and under such hallucinations? And at this point there is nothing I so freely wonder at as the fact that there is no one on the whole Sorbonne faculty who has discovered the view of Augustine and, if you please, it is by this argument that a book was edited by one or two Sophists under the fabricated name of the faculty.

Nor with any greater trustworthiness do those French Sorbonners judge the view of Ambrose, since it is agreed that in the entire disputation the author of the book *On the Calling of the Gentiles*, whoever he is, says that those things which are done without grace are sins. When declaring what kind of grace he is talking about, he produces among other witnesses this one also which has been quoted in the Epistle to the Hebrews from Jeremiah: "I will give my law in their inward parts and will write it upon their hearts." It is so far from being the case that these words can be twisted, either into special Sorbonnic aid or into gratuitous gifts, that scarcely any other passage of Scripture describes more suitably the grace given through Christ which you call the grace that makes one pleasing to God.

It is not still obscure, is it, both in what manner Luther has quoted Augustine and Ambrose and what the Sorbonne resembles, which we perceive here is so crassly in error that those at Louvain and Cologne have never been more crassly foolish? O wretched France, to have been polluted by such censors and judges of sacred matters, who are really more worthy to deal with sewers than to treat sacred letters!

From this view on free will follow those things which Luther has written about contrition and therefore about repentance in general. But, oh, how wretched are we who now for almost four hundred years have had no writer in the church to set forth the right and proper form of repentance! Feigned contritions have been imposed upon some, and the consciences of others have been tormented by satisfactions. Now, finally, the mercy of God has looked down upon us and has revealed the Gospel to his people and has raised up the consciences of those whom he has called.

If you ask what Luther has conferred upon the church, you have right here the sum of the matter. He has taught the true way of repentance, and likewise he has shown the use of the sacraments. And as witnesses in this matter I have the consciences of many. But I do not here wish to dispute about the forms of repentance or about the Sacraments, since those Sorbonners have only condemned Luther, but indeed have not conquered him either by reason or by Scripture.

But the truth of Lutheran doctrine stands unshaken and immovable not only against those Sorbonners but also against the rulers of darkness. If they will use the judgments of Scripture in opposing the things Luther has taught, we shall in no way hesitate to defend his teachings. For this doctrine of Luther about repentance will never be wrested from my heart or from the heart of any of the faithful by any force, not even Sorbonnic or papal.

Of what importance is it again to admonish about the law and the councils, when I have shown plainly above that in these matters Luther agrees with the ancients? Nevertheless, in order for you to see how boldly the Sorbonnic Sophists dispose of the divine law, it is agreeable to go back to this point, as it were, by the right of return. The law about not taking revenge, they say, is too burden-

some for Christian law. O wicked Sophists, who measure the burden
of a law by the philosophy of Aristotle! Is that not a burden on
human nature, the law against concupiscence? Is it to be abrogated
therefore, according to the Sorbonnic Sophists? Is that burdensome
law about loving God alone to be abrogated because it is a burden?
O unbalanced, wicked men, that statement relates to you which
says: "He who has broken one of the least of the commands will be
least in the kingdom of heaven."

And why did you not think the same when you made precepts
about satisfactions? Are they not a burden for a conscience afflicted
in itself? But you indeed are both devising new burdens and abro-
gating those which have been divinely imposed. Thus it is fitting for
you to fulfill prophetic Scripture and to strengthen the wicked man
and to afflict the heart of the just man. And to teach briefly, omitting many things, the passage in 1 Corinthians 6 is clear that it is
demanded and not counseled that we not seek revenge: "Now to
be sure, it is altogether a fault, that you have judgments at law
with one another." But if it is a fault to reclaim one's property by
judgment, there is no doubt that the law demands that we do not
take vengeance.

Christian reader, I have wanted to warn you of these things
lest you be frightened away from the Lutheran doctrine by the
authority of the Sorbonne, the wisdom of whose position you have
already learned from various passages discussed here. And from
those passages which I have noted, you will evaluate the rest.
For the Sorbonne is like unto itself. And you may find Christ
among the carpenters far more quickly than in that class of men.
In the meantime, it is your duty to demand along with me that
Paris give the reason for its judgment. When it has published that,
we shall give a fuller discussion of our own views. Farewell.

Wittenberg.

The disputations contained in this list of theses were held on July 25, 1522. The person who responded to Melanchthon was Philip Eberbach, later a schoolmaster in Joachimthal and in Koburg. At this time it was popular to discuss spiritual and worldly government. Since Luther's return from the Wartburg comparative peace had been restored, but still the discussions about types of government were the vogue. In these thirty-four theses we get a glimpse of Melanchthon as a social and political philosopher.[1]

CHAPTER SEVEN

THEMES FOR THE SIXTH HOLIDAY
1522

1. Government is twofold: spiritual and physical.

2. Physical government regulates with respect to the external control of affairs.

3. Then, too, there is civil administration, which coerces the body, makes divisions of property, and prohibits violence.

4. God entrusted corporal government to Adam when he subjected Eve to him and ordered homicides to be killed.

5. This law was subsequently confirmed, both by the law of retaliation and by the precept: Honor thy father and thy mother.

6. In like manner it was enjoined upon parents by divine right to rule their family corporally.

7. That law which establishes the right to kill a stiff-necked son testifies of that very thing (Deuteronomy 21).

8. For since the Law of God does not justify, therefore ordinances of the flesh have been handed down in the Law.

9. For this external administration is the righteousness of the flesh.

10. There are those persons who stand in the place of parents, to whom the latter entrust their duty, such as teachers, magistrates in the cities, princes, to whom, by consent of the citizens, the rule is committed.

11. That is what Paul means in Romans 13 by the word government when he calls it the power ordained of God.

12. For the orderly arrangement is from God, of whatever kind they may be, who either seize power or wield it.

13. When I mention magistrates or princes, I include all servants of the laws, judges, advocates, all defenders of litigants.

14. The servants of the laws can use this orderly arrangement without sin, since it is a good creation of God.

15. They sin who take up the sword against this government and are of the same kind as those who seize the possessions of others.

16. Even Peter was sinning when he took up the sword against duly constituted authority.

17. For Christ also confirms the right of the sword when he says: "He who takes the sword ought to perish by the sword."

18. Jehu did not sin when he took arms against the king, for he was compelled by a clearly divine call to do what he did.

19. Zimri sinned when he invaded the kingdom without a definite call.

20. Legal government, since it is of God, cannot be violated unless God commands it.

21. In the spiritual realm, the Word of God alone rules, not human power.

22. Ecclesiastical traditions are civil laws, of some value pedagogically, but pertaining in no way to spiritual government.

23. I am speaking, however, of those traditions in which nothing has been decreed contrary to Scripture.

24. The Word of God gives life to some, slays others, since it judges the world. Thus Peter rightly kills Ananias.

25. The ministry of the Gospel is plainly a spiritual realm.

26. Because this ministry proclaims nothing but the righteousness of the Spirit, it lays down nothing about the external control of affairs.

27. For the righteousness of the Spirit is life eternal, for the Word is life (John 1).

28. But what is the concern of life eternal with the righteousness of the flesh, which is concerned with things that perish in the using?

29. They are miserably deceived who judge that the righteousness of the Spirit is nothing other than that carnal righteousness of the world.

30. Since ignorance and contempt for God can stand along with the righteousness of the world, that righteousness is not life.

31. But there are certain external matters which even the saints use, such as food and drink.

32. Those who are justified by the Spirit cannot abuse external matters.

33. Accordingly, corporal government has been instituted for the coercions of the bodies of those who are without the Spirit of God.

34. In brief, the righteousness of the world is not life, but death and the penalty of sin.

PHIL. MEL. 1522

Joachim Camerarius in his "Life of Melanchthon"[1] gives us a detailed account of the occasion for the composition of this writing. On his return from Bretten, where he had visited relatives, Melanchthon, not far from Frankfurt, met the twenty-year-old Landgrave Philip of Hesse. The prince constrained the young professor to spend the night in his lodge and proceeded to ask him many questions. The next day he let Melanchthon go on condition that he write the prince a detailed composition on the questions which were current.

Melanchthon immediately fulfilled the wish of the landgrave. He presented the fundamental points and at the same time discussed the distinctive elements of Luther's doctrine. O. Clemen[2] thinks that it was written in May of 1524 and that it reminds one in particular places of the "Judgment to Campegius." But since Melanchthon returned to Wittenberg on June 8, 1524, we shall have to reckon with a date in June. This writing was published twice in the very same year, first in Latin and then in German. How much in demand the German translation was can be seen from the fact that three translations of it appeared in Wittenberg, Erfurt, and Augsburg.[3]

CHAPTER EIGHT

SUMMARY OF DOCTRINE

1524

To the Most Illustrious Prince of Hesse, Greetings from Philip Melanchthon.

There have always been varied opinions concerning religion or the Gospel, as Paul declares when he complains that to the Jews it seemed a stumbling block, and to the Greeks, foolishness. Then, among those who seem to embrace religion there are some who have been so induced by considerations of the stomach. For while a goodly number of bishops and the princes are patronizing the office of the pontiff for the sake of private convenience, we see that many of the people are in favor of Luther as though he were the author of freedom; they are disgusted with the old practices. Ambition or the hope of gain is attracting some professors to teach a kind of new doctrine in order to sell themselves to the people, and hypocrisy incites a few to hold on to the doctrine of works. By far the fewest number, from the fear of divine judgment, desire both to learn the dogmas of religion and to follow them in ordering their lives.

Furthermore, since Christ is offended by no sin as he is by contempt for the Gospel, care must be taken that whatever you may decide to do in "the Luther affair," as they call it, it may not obstruct the glory of the Gospel. It is well known what threat Christ makes against blasphemers when he says: "Whoever shall fall upon this rock shall be broken, and upon whom this rock falls he shall be ground to pieces." Moreover, Scripture should be consulted in such matters, as is enjoined in Isaiah 8: "To the law and to the testimony." The almost depraved customs of our ancestors, the badly understood writings of the fathers, and fallacious judgment of reason are brought up to judge this controversy. Paul assuredly calls us back to Scripture when he says that Scripture is divinely inspired for the purpose of teaching, reproving, and instructing us about those things which relate to piety. And Peter orders us to follow Scripture as a shining light before us in this darkness.

There are two topics which are principally discussed at this particular time. The first is: Wherein does Christian righteousness consist? The second is: What is to be thought about human traditions? There are very many, however, who think that the controversy is not about an actual reality, but about mere words, and that the contentions are being engaged in beyond the point of necessity by foolish or even ambitious men. But when the situation has been interpreted, it will be clear that there have been great, serious and necessary reasons for the renewal of ecclesiastical doctrine. And so I shall speak of the former topic, wherein I feel Christian righteousness or true piety consists.

At the end of Luke's Gospel Christ enjoins that repentance and the remission of sins be proclaimed to all peoples. From this it can be deduced just what the Gospel is or what that righteousness is which is to become known to the world by the ministry of Christ and of the apostles. Accordingly, the Gospel is the preaching of repentance and of the remission of sins. It is truly Christian righteousness when a confused conscience is lifted up by faith in Christ and feels that it receives the remission of sins for Christ's sake. This is not brought about by feigning repentance or trust. Rather, since the Gospel teaches the truth, it condems hypocrisy and pretense both in repentance and in trust. But the Holy Spirit reveals sin in human hearts, terrifies and confounds consciences, and incites them to believe the promises of Christ, who both made satisfaction for our sins and promises us the remission of sins.

Neither that fear of divine judgment nor the trust by which the conscience is raised up and made serene is actually assumed, unless the Holy Spirit moves the hearts. In what manner this is done is declared by Christ in John 6: "No man cometh to me unless the Father draws him." And Isaiah says: "It does not mount up into the heart of man, etc." And Paul declares: "The natural man does not perceive the things which are of the Spirit of God." For although you may hear the divine threats and promises, nevertheless the heart does not give assent, however you may pretend, unless the Holy Spirit has taken possession. In favorable circumstances we dream that God is too lenient to be able to be very angry with us. In moments of adversity we think that he is too cruel to have regard for us, however much you implore aid from him. And finally, never indeed do we seriously and truly think that we are in God's care, just as those persons in Ezekiel 7 said: "The Lord does not see us; the Lord has deserted the earth." Accordingly, the Holy Spirit, after revealing sin and the judgment of God, strikes terror into our consciences by the preaching of repentance. And he lifts them up again through the Gospel, that is, through the announcement of the remission of sins.

Next, when the heart has recognized both the power of God's wrath and the might of his mercy, just then it finally conceives a true opinion of God by which it entrusts itself to him, hopes, throws itself upon him in adversity, and fears him. At last it recognizes that God not only sees us, but also judges and saves us. In this manner does the Holy Spirit bring forth faith in our hearts, the fear of God, rejection of self, chastity, modesty, and other fruits enumerated in Galatians 5. And that is done which was foretold by Jeremiah: The law is inscribed, not on tables of stone, but by the finger of God upon the heart. This, briefly, is evangelical or Christian righteousness: When our conscience is confounded, we are raised up by faith in Christ through whom we recognize the power of God's mercy. In John 17 Christ defined eternal life: "This is life eternal, that they know thee, the only true God, and Jesus Christ whom thou hast sent."

Moreover, life eternal is that very righteousness which the Gospel declares and which Christ places simply in the knowledge of the Father and of himself. Nor indeed is that a knowledge of God which hypocrisy and human reason feign when they invoke the name of God. Nor likewise is that a knowledge of God which is commonly taught, namely, to know his commands, or in one way or another to pretend. For the Jews knew the name of God, they knew the Law, and they imitated like monkeys. Nevertheless, Christ denies that they know God when he says in John 8: "It is my Father who glorifies me of whom ye say, 'He is our God,' but ye have not known him." Those who truly know him, when they really fear his judgment, are raised up in adversity so as safely to await help from him. For faith produces tranquillity in the heart and a sense of security, which surely the powers of free will in no way can surpass.

Nevertheless, this is the truest worship of God, according to

Psalm 50: "Call upon me in the day of tribulation and I will save thee and thou wilt glorify me." He does not call masses or other little ceremonies or works a true worship of God. But calling upon him in adversity is a true worship. In adversity reason feels plainly that it is neglected and not noticed by God. Faith incites the heart to think well of God and to think that God does care for it.

In some manner I have represented wherein Christian or evangelical righteousness consists. I know, however, that these things seem partly obscure and partly ridiculous. What you experience, Paul foretold a long time ago, saying that to the Jews the Gospel seemed a stumbling block, and to the Gentiles, foolishness. Let those who laugh at these things know that Christ will judge blasphemers and will mete out punishment to them. Since he declared beforehand in overturned Jerusalem how angry he was with blasphemers, he will not close his eyes to our impiety.

See, moreover, how much comfort there is in this proclamation for miserable consciences when they understand that it is the truest possible righteousness to believe that through Christ our sins are forgiven without our own satisfaction, without our own merits. I have known some who had clearly thrown away all hope of salvation before they discovered this teaching because their conscience could not be lifted by satisfactions and feigned works. These persons, after the Gospel had illuminated the world much more clearly, again with a strong spirit conceived the hope of salvation, and not only the hope but also the power or strength against sins. The only thing that mattered was rightly to know the Gospel. Many are offended when they hear so much attributed to faith and prefer that works be demanded. We are not speaking of that faith which reason feigns and which is common to all of the people, but of a true knowledge of God which produces fear and other good works. Besides, we require repentance which, if only it is not feigned, certainly recalls us from evil works. This righteousness which I have described is required by Christ. Ceremonies and the like he does not demand when he says: "The kingdom of God is within you." Wherefore, he has not demanded the ceremonies of Moses but has made us free to use our ceremony, namely, the Eucharist, when we wish.

Human Righteousness

Paul says that faith is not the property of all persons. Wherefore, Christian righteousness is not common to all but is the possession of the few whom God calls, as it were, out of the world. What, therefore, should one do, you will say, about those who do not possess Christian righteousness? Shall they sin and dare to do all things with impunity until God transforms them? By no means, for Paul teaches that the Law was founded for the unrighteous.

Accordingly, besides Christian righteousness there is human righteousness, by which the wicked should be coerced. This type of righteousness I customarily call "pedagogy," following the custom of Paul, who says in Galatians 3 that the Law is a schoolmaster to Christ, and that a young child ought to be under the Law as though under teachers until he grows up in Christ.

This training of the state is a certain righteousness which forms character and contains rites and human and civil duties. It accustoms children to the worship of God by teaching and exercise, and restrains foolish people from vices, just as Solomon also teaches in Proverbs 26: "A whip for the horse, a bridle for the ass, and a rod for the fool's back." And Proverbs 23: "Withhold not discipline from a child, for if thou beatest him with a rod, he shall not die." To this point relates also the right of the sword, which as Paul says, ought to be a terror for the wicked and an honor for the good.

This political righteousness is wisely to be distinguished from religion or evangelical righteousness. But many today are preaching evangelical righteousness in such a way that a new wickedness is being born. For some wicked persons are feigning faith and are glorying in the name of Christ and conceiving a certain kind of carnal security by which they are being precipitated into great crimes, and they think that they ought not to be coerced. Both the training of children is being neglected and other things of this nature, although God has nevertheless subjected to this schooling all who either are not in Christ or are weak, according to the position of Paul in Galatians 3 and 4. In the Law there was a command to inscribe the Decalogue upon the entrances of homes and likewise on the fringes of garments. What else were such duties as these but a pedagogy that coerced and restrained children and those like them? The multitude must be instructed, ruled, and coerced in this manner even now by laws and certain duties. And I am of the opinion that formerly with this counsel monasteries were founded to instruct young children according to this type of pedagogy. But such a pedagogy, although divinely ordered, nevertheless does not justify one before God, but, as Paul says, constitutes the beggarly elements of the world. That is, they are regulations which serve human need but do not merit grace or remission of sins, or that the Holy Spirit should come. For thus Paul says in Ephesians 2: "Ye are saved by grace through faith . . ." On the contrary, when the opinion grew that this is Christian righteousness, a great mistake was made. For we see to what degree this pedagogy has been turned into a wicked and feigned worship of God in the monasteries.

So far I have set forth my opinion. It remains to point out where it differs from that of the Aristotelian theologians, which I shall do, but very briefly. They teach that we merit grace by our own powers and our own effort and that sins are remitted for the sake of our own satisfactions. By these dogmas the satisfaction by Christ is plainly obscured. Moreover, what solace or hope does the conscience have if salvation depends on our merits and not on grace through Christ? Almost in the same manner they do not need the Holy Spirit in repentance or in justification, but are content with the efforts of reason. These, nevertheless, teach nothing except unadulterated hypocrisy, as Paul declares when he says: "It has not entered into the heart of man . . ." Likewise, "All are without the glory of God."

From this it can be recognized whether the controversy is over words or an actual reality. The Gospel for the sake of Christ raises up consciences by the gracious remission of sins, while the Aristotelians by their doctrine of merits actually plunge them into despair. The Gospel teaches that hearts are cleansed and renewed by the Holy Spirit so that they know God, trust God, and fear God, while the Aristotelians think that these things can be accomplished by hypocritical reason. But this is an obscure distinction because it cannot be discerned with the eyes of the flesh.

Human Traditions

Although the former topic is more obscure than the argument about human traditions, I still do not know why it is that this dispute incites greater disturbances in the world. And although Luther urges the more those things which I have said above about repentance—the free remission of sins, faith, hope—and admonishes that in these is the sum of religion, nevertheless there are not a few who think that Luther is teaching nothing but contempt for human traditions. And these persons think they are very pious when they have raved strongly against the priests and have eaten meats contrary to custom. I shall briefly set forth my own view.

The Lord says in Isaiah that in vain he is worshipped by the commandments of men, and this statement was repeated by Christ in Matthew. Therefore it is an act of wickedness to institute any human tradition or to preserve it in the place of the worship of God as if you are justified by its observance. Christ's statement is quite clear that he is worshipped in vain by the commandments of men. But there are some traditions that can be kept without doing any sin, such as those that have been instituted about vestments or foods or similar minor matters. It is enough to feel about them as the Gospel says—when kept, they do not justify. Nor do they do any harm when neglected. This agrees with Paul's statement: "Be ye not vexed with decrees." Nevertheless, in pursuit of peace it would be important for them to be kept in a civil manner, according to the rule: "If anyone asks you to go one mile, go two." Likewise, he who has been called in circumcision let him not seek uncircumcision, and he who is called in uncircumcision, let him not seek circumcision.

There are, indeed, other traditions which cannot be kept without sin. And of this kind is that unclean celibacy so cruelly and wickedly demanded by the pope. But Christ denies that celibacy is given to all. And Paul has written that it is better to marry than to burn. Hence they do not in any way hinder this tradition whose powers do not endure celibacy. For no human tradition can be instituted against the Word of God. It is not given to all. Nor do vows avail in those things which cannot be discharged without sin. For what if you have vowed that you will commit murder? Moreover, there is sin in the vows of those who cannot fulfill celibacy or who, by that monastic observance, think that they are justified. Therefore they should be rescinded, especially since Paul openly teaches that they are lying spirits who prohibit marriage. But among these spirits are the princes, lictors, and satellites who keep the pope's law. As Micah says, "the prince demands and the judge obeys." O wretched conspiracy! O what a calamitous compact! Although the princes see that the pope is publicly at war with God, although they see that religion simply is openly despised by him, yet they are not moved to look to their own salvation rather than serve his madness. Their hearts undoubtedly are stony, to have no care at all for the will of God.

There remains the mass, concerning which it is of no consequence to dispute at this time since not even the papists themselves can approve of the trafficking in masses and the character of those who are profaning the Mass. And yet they do not permit this to be corrected.

You know what I think about the renewed ecclesiastical doctrine. Nor have I been afraid that you should unpleasantly bear having these things written to you, since it is befitting to know the judgment of anyone about religion. Moreover, you have ordered me to write to you in full whether anyone would sin if he did not use the Eucharist. But I could not conveniently speak about the use of ceremonies and about that liberty which gives us the right to use or not to use ceremonies, unless I included the whole situation.

Now I have thought it to be my duty also to advise you about those things which seem to be of importance both for your salvation and for the public tranquillity. Horace bids us to look even if a blind man wants to show us the way. Wherefore I beg you also that it may not inconvenience you to become thoroughly acquainted with whatever thoughts I, surely with pious study, have written out for you. You see how the whole world is being afflicted with dangerous dissension. And, too, the contest is almost solely about ceremonies and human traditions in which, if the princes were to permit somewhat sane counsels, peace could be restored. Sometimes both sides are being irritated by seditious demagogues. Indeed, those who patronize the pope only embitter the souls of men by their wicked discourses and pamphlets. And some pseudo-Lutherans, while otherwise gratifying the desire of the masses for new things, are everywhere exciting seditions by their profane and seditious outcries. For it can never be but that the name of the Gospel is assigned as a pretext for personal cupidities.

I have seen some persons who denied that the magistrates, or those to whom the magistrates assign them, should be responsible for the state tithes and other things. Meanwhile, such demagogues are arising on both sides, while the princes, by their honorable counsels, cease to offer aid to the state. For those who attempt simply to suppress the Gospel will not accomplish anything. The Gospel is such that human force cannot suppress it. Again, those who either out of fear or folly grant too much to the masses do not advance the Gospel but nourish the fury of the masses into a public calamity. And when the masses abuse the Word of God, they injure the glory of the Gospel more than those who oppose it. Therefore the princes ought to provide the means for teaching the Gospel, which, when it is rightly proclaimed, teaches peace and order and does not incite seditions. And they should restrain the fury of the masses who, under a wicked pretext of the Gospel, are raising a tumult and are threatening to make an attack upon the fortunes of others.

For the princes bear arms for this purpose: to be a terror to evil works, to use Paul's words. The gift of God is peace, and this excellent gift cannot be preserved if, to abolish the Gospel, the princes should alienate God from themselves. The sacred histories commend King Jehoshaphat because he appointed Levites to teach religion. Following his example, the princes ought to provide for moderate and good men to teach sacred things. Nor must children be neglected, because that age of public activity is just like a seed bed. All the protections required by religion or by children's training should be preserved with greatest care. These matters require a longer treatise, but I have been rather brief, since I have thought that you had need only to be reminded of certain things. Therefore I commend to your conscience the cause of religion. If you have reason for it, may you imitate Jehoshaphat rather than Pharaoh.

Moreover, I desire that Christ may abundantly supply you with his Spirit and with the will to counsel in the best possible manner for your own salvation and that of the state, so that you may not delay the course of the Gospel or be cruel toward those whom necessity of conscience sometimes forces to depart from the laws of the pontiff.

In the course of the year 1527 the disturbances of "fanatic spirits," as Melanchthon called the Anabaptists, took on more serious forms. Melanchthon regarded this phenomenon and its eruption in the church as very dangerous. As he wrote to Jerome Baumgartner on October 23, 1527, he had finally decided to write "Contra Anabaptistas," and with this he entered into the situation. But illness and other reasons prevented him from completing his plan.[1] Spalatin and Camerarius also shared his plan.[2] Jonas, in the foreword to this translation, which was dedicated to Michael Meinenburg, feels that this writing is the foundation of Melanchthon's lectures.

During the period of the Visitation of the Churches Melanchthon had already prepared a short judgment about infant baptism but had not published it. From the foreword, dated May 10, 1528, and dedicated to the Abbot Friedrich Pistorius of St. Aegidius Cloister, with whom Melanchthon lived in May 1526, it appears that this little book must have been finished several months prior to this date. Actually, Melanchthon reported the conclusion of his work on January 23, 1528.[3] On October 12, 1528, he informs us that Pistorius had received the work.[4]

At first the writing appeared by itself in Wittenberg in 1528, then together with the "Visitation Articles" and a "Judgment of John Brenz" and again with the "Judgment of Brenz" in Frankfurt in 1562.

Since this whole question of re-baptism was actual and widespread among the people, Justus Jonas made a translation of it into German at Wittenberg in 1528. This translation enjoyed wide circulation. In October 1528 there appeared in Marburg a further translation to which the judgment of J. Brenz was appended. In addition, there was also an edition released in Erfurt.[5] The first Latin edition is not contained in Bretschneider's "Corpus Reformatorum" series. Nor does the Basle edition of Melanchthon's works printed in 1541 contain it.

CHAPTER NINE

AGAINST THE ANABAPTISTS

1528

To the Reverend Father Friedrich Pistorius,
Abbot of Saint Aegidius of Nürnberg.
Greetings from Philip Melanchthon.

Several months ago I wrote a short argument against the Anabaptists. For I was so busy at that time that I did not have the opportunity to address myself at length to that one argument. But those who were asking for my judgment were so urgent that it did not seem that they would leave sufficient free time for a longer commentary. Nevertheless, I permitted that this writing, of whatever quality it might be, be published in order that in the meantime my opinion might be on record. This dogma drags along with it many pests, and these fanatical men are in error not merely in one respect. That is what I have lately learned from a certain fellow who was initiated into these wicked rites, but who of his own accord has returned to his senses.

There is not one of the ancient heresies which does not seem to sprout forth again with these authors. Therefore it is profitable to exhort unwary men to flee the Anabaptists. "Satan walketh to and fro as a roaring lion, seeking whom he may devour." For what else are their arguments but diabolical snares? Not often do they cite the Scriptures, but for the most part rely upon reasoning, and this reasoning is indeed quite inconsistent. This is the judgment of corrupt minds, to use Paul's words. But let us pray Christ, who said to Peter that he had prayed for him that his faith fail not, both to guard our hearts and stir up faith in us lest we be dragged away

from the simple Word of God to wicked opinions. May you be
abundantly well!

I have often said at other times just what topics it is most necessary to know. Now Christ pointed them out when he ordered that
"repentance and the remission of sins are to be declared." And
Paul intended to show what the chief points of Christian doctrine
are when he said: "The end of the law is love from a pure heart
and a good conscience and faith unfeigned." These same topics
are set forth in the prophets: "I have desired mercy, not sacrifice,
and a knowledge of God more than burnt offerings."

In this manner and in other passages Scripture often admonishes
us especially to know these topics: the doctrine of repentance and
likewise of faith, patience, love, and all good works. We ought to
look into these topics and our hearts should be stirred and exercised
by them, so that simultaneously fear and faith may be increased
within us and the knowledge of God may grow. And as often as
we take any part of Scripture into our hands, the topics I have
enumerated should be especially sought out. Moreover, a summary
of Christian doctrine must be sketched. But in this age men take
delight in a certain wisdom which is plainly absurd and wrangle
about ceremonies and likewise about human traditions without any
end. In the meantime, there is great silence about repentance, faith,
the cross, love, and all good works. But at other times I have often
discussed the sum of Christian doctrine, and perhaps we shall take
it up again in its proper place.

Now, since there are so many dangerous dissensions about the
Sacraments, it seems best in this place for us to touch upon these
controversies, to fortify the inexperienced beforehand in some manner against heresies which are arising in great numbers from that
source. For it is difficult to hold on to the truth in the midst of so
many offences, in the midst of so many dissensions, and it has
almost come to pass that error is begetting error. And to what
degree this is true is signified also by Paul, when he says that
heretics progress from bad to worse.

What Is a Sacrament?

Now a sacrament is a divinely instituted sign of the promised
grace of God. A saying of long standing appeals to me: "Let the
Word be added to the element and it becomes a Sacrament." For
these are the two parts of a Sacrament: a thing which signifies

promised grace, and the Word by which grace is promised and by which God has instituted the sign. Therefore many Sacraments could be named if anyone should want to collect diligently all the signs of divine promises. Affliction is a sacrament, for it is a thing to which God has joined the Word by which he promises his grace, such as: "When we are judged we are being chastened by God lest we should be damned with this world." Similarly: "He reproves the son whom he loves." Likewise: "Call upon me in the day of tribulation and I will save thee."

Therefore, although our carnal sense protests and judges that affliction is a sign of wrath, we should nevertheless decide, not in accordance with our carnal sense, but in accordance with the Word of God, whether the affliction is a sign of grace or of mercy. Likewise, the duties of charity are sacraments because the Word of God is added, by which grace is promised: "Give and it shall be given unto you." "To him that forgiveth it shall be forgiven." For just as the rainbow is the sign that the earth will no more be destroyed by a flood, so the works of charity signify that God wants to pardon us. Just as Gideon's fleece was the sign of promised victory, so is affliction the sign of promised grace. Nevertheless, as the fleece did not justify Gideon, but his faith by which he believed God, likewise affliction does not justify. Nor do the works of charity, for they are only signs of promised grace. Therefore faith must be added, a faith that believes the promises of God. In this manner many other things also could be collected to which the promises of grace have been added and which can be rightfully and usefully called Sacraments. But by common usage we recognize only these two Sacraments, Baptism and the Lord's Supper, because they are ceremonies which have been divinely instituted and to which have been added the promises of grace.

After I have spoken about the word "sacrament," I must also speak in general about the use of the Sacraments. In the first place, therefore, we should know this, that the Sacraments have not been instituted merely for the purpose of being marks to distinguish Christians from Gentiles, as the toga distinguished Romans from Greeks or as the vesture distinguishes monks. Some do write that Sacraments have been instituted that we may show the Gentiles through them that we believe in Christ and that we may profess our faith before men and by our example invite others to take up the doctrine of Christ. But we should feel that Sacraments are signs of the divine will toward us and not merely signs of our profession toward men. For the fleece was to Gideon, not merely a mark by which his army would be distinguished from the enemy, as if by some signal of the camp, but rather it was a sign of the will of God and a pledge of promised victory. So, also for us, the Sacraments are signs of God's will, as Christ also teaches when he says: "Do this in remembrance of me." To remember Christ is not only to teach others, but also to remember the benefits which we ourselves have received from him through his death and resurrection, that is, the remission of sins which we receive through him. As the will of God is shown in the Word or in the promise, so also is it shown in a sign as in a picture. As the Word is perceived in our ears to arouse faith in our hearts, so a sign occurs to our eyes that it may also arouse faith in our hearts. Therefore Augustine wrote that a Sacrament is the visible Word, because it signifies the same thing as the promise does, and is, as it were, a picture of the divine will, just as the Word is the voice of the divine will.

It is my conviction that the reader should be admonished in this way about the use of the Sacraments, because some are teaching that the only use of Sacraments is to profess our faith before men. They pass by this part, that we must use them because they admonish and signify what we receive from God, since they raise up and stir up faith in our hearts. This topic, however, will be clearer when we have interpreted the proper use of both of these Sacraments.

In the second instance, it is profitable also to point out that the Sacraments do not justify. For they are in error who think that they merit the remission of sins by this work, when they eat the Lord's Supper. Paul teaches that we are justified not by works but by faith. And just as hearing the Word without faith does not justify, so using a Sacrament without faith does not justify. For even the Sacrament itself is, as I have said before, some sort of visible Word. Just as the voice is perceived by our ears, so the Sacrament confronts our eyes to move our hearts to believe. And since the Sacraments contain promises, so finally we use them correctly when we believe that we attain those things which are promised, for promises require faith, as Paul teaches in Romans 4. In that same passage he teaches that Abraham was not justified because of circumcision, but circumcision was a sign of righteousness, that is, a sign by which God bore witness that he had mercy on Abraham and justified him. By this testimony Abraham's faith, by which he was justified, was strengthened and nourished. Therefore Paul calls circumcision the seal of righteousness. For as seals make us certain of the will of another, so through circumcision Abraham was made more certain of God's will. Thus we also should use the Sacraments and believe that they are signs of righteousness which Christ has presented to us to witness that he forgives us our sins and justifies us. Because we have been baptized we carry the sign by which Christ witnesses that he forgives those who repent or whose consciences are terrified, not otherwise than if he should testify the same thing daily by some new sign from heaven. Nor must it be imagined that baptism is for one time. We always carry this mark, both of repentance and of promised grace.

Baptism

Baptism is the sign of repentance and of the remission of sins. For in the beginning the fact that it is the sign of repentance is witnessed by John in Matthew 3 when he says: "I baptize you with water unto repentance." The preaching of John is a preaching of repentance. Thus it is written in Isaiah 40. Baptism is also a sign of that word which was preached by John. That Baptism is a sign of the remission of sins is clear from Christ's words: "He that believeth and is baptized shall be saved." And Paul calls Baptism a washing of regeneration and the renewal of the Holy Spirit. Baptism therefore is not a sign of mortification only, especially since the preaching of repentance in the Gospel is not only a threatening, but has the promise of grace joined to it. John says: "Repent ye, for the kingdom of heaven is nigh." And John 1: "Behold the Lamb of God that taketh away the sins of the world."

Therefore Baptism does not signify repentance without at the same time declaring the remission of sins throughout the whole life time, as Paul says: "As many as were baptized in Christ Jesus were baptized into his death. For we are buried with him by baptism into death." Since, then, Baptism signifies mortification or repentance, and these things should be done throughout our whole life until we die, it is quite agreed that Baptism is not a work that pertains to one certain period but signifies repentance during our whole life. Therefore there is no necessity at all to seek again for a sign; otherwise it would be necessary to be baptized daily. We ought always to repent and to be alarmed at the judgment of God. We ought always to be raised up and confirmed through faith.

The Use and the Fruit of the Sacrament of Baptism

In this manner, then, Baptism ought to be used. It should terrify us and exhort us to repentance and reveal the wrath of God against sin. And since we are baptized into Christ, it entreats us to see in Christ the wrath of God against sin. For God is so enraged at sin that no creature, no angel, no good works of any saint whatsoever could destroy sin. Likewise, as he has willed his own Son to be offered for sins, "so that not only should he be afflicted outside the gate by such a kind of death, but that suffering also from within, as though cast off by God, he might be terrified."

Accordingly, since God so greatly hates sin, we should be admonished by Baptism, which has buried us with Christ into death, truly to be afraid and terrified by the magnitude of divine wrath, just as Christ also says of his death: "Weep not for me but weep for yourselves and your children." For he transfers the reason and the example of his death to us, as if to say: "I suffer, but for you; I bear the wrath of God, not that I have deserved but which you deserve. Unless you weep and repent, you will be punished and the wrath of God will abide upon you."

Therefore this is the use of Baptism: to be frightened by the magnitude of divine wrath to follow the example of Christ. They defile Baptism who live securely without fear of God and without repentance, even if they were washed daily. Once and for all, Baptism is a sign handed down to us of the judgment of God and of our own death. Accordingly, there is no need to renew the sign itself. Let us look back to that to which the sign relates. We have received, as though condemned to death, a sign of our death and of God's judgment. Therefore we ought to be afraid and repent and feel that God by right should be angry with us and punish us. Nor is it enough to be thoroughly terrified by Baptism, but in these terrors we must take hold of faith and consider Baptism and feel that it is a sign of promised grace and of the remission of sins. We ought to apprehend the voice of John, "The kingdom of heaven is nigh," that is, grace, wisdom, mercy, righteousness, and life. Likewise: "Behold the Lamb of God who taketh away the sins of the world."

As often as the conscience labors and contends with despair, we ought to contemplate this mark of the will and mercy of God, which is a testimony of promised grace, provided we believe in the God who promises. And this faith that so raises us up in these anxieties is righteousness before God. God demands this faith and it thinks well of God. It sees that we are loved by God, that God cares for us as a Father for the sake of Christ. Therefore Baptism is to be so used even for the purpose of consolation. And, just as the Word has been handed down to be a bulkwark against despair, so Baptism also must be numbered among the weapons which have been handed down for those fighting with despair and unbelief. Baptism ought to confirm us in our faith just as if new miracles from heaven were to be revealed to us. And, just as the fleece aroused Gideon to believe, so Baptism ought to urge and arouse us also to believe.

In the second place, it should be observed here that since Baptism is a sign of mortification, all afflictions, including even death itself, are signified by Baptism. And it has been handed down for this purpose, to testify that afflictions, as well as death, which has been imposed upon human nature because of sin, are now salutary. We are not afflicted in order to be destroyed but to be saved, and our afflictions have been mingled with the death of Christ.

Just as the death of Christ is a sacrifice, so are our afflictions sacrifices pleasing to God, since they have been joined to Christ through faith. As Christ has been glorified, so Baptism signifies and testifies that we are heard, liberated, assisted, and glorified. Therefore, in all of our afflictions, we ought to look back upon Baptism which admonishes us that it is pleasing to God that we are humbled and afflicted, and it signifies that aid is promised us in all of our afflictions.

The Baptism of John and of Christ

The external Baptism which John administered differed in no way from the external Baptism administered by Christ or the apostles. For the same sign was instituted divinely through the ministry of John, who is a minister of the New Testament, as Christ said: "The law and the prophets until John . . ." Therefore Christ himself used a sign that had already been instituted. John, moreover, does not distinguish his external Baptism but his ministry from the office of Christ, because John baptizes with water only, that is, he administers external Baptism and preaches the Word, just as the apostles do.

But Christ not only administers external Baptism but makes satisfaction for our sins, takes away sins, and gives the Holy Spirit. Therefore the external sign administered by Christ differs in no way from the sign administered by John, both signifying and accomplishing the same thing, but their persons and offices differ. John was sent only to preach, as were the apostles. Christ, however, was sent to take away sins and to give the Holy Spirit. Therefore John signified that sin is not destroyed by our own works or satisfactions. He taught that we cannot become the sons of God unless Christ sends into our hearts the Holy Spirit, by whom we are sanctified and renewed and governed. Just as the external Word is the same, no matter who proclaims it, whether John, or Christ, or the apostles, so also is the sign the same. But this is distinctively a work of Christ, to give the Holy Spirit. Moreover, the Holy Spirit is given when God, either by Word or sign, terrifies and consoles and quickens our hearts. For both the Word and the sign are used that God through them may move our hearts, thoroughly terrify, and again raise up through faith, when our hearts contemplate either the Word or the sign. It is profitable for us to hold fast and to know these things about the use of Baptism in order that we may not dream that Baptism is a work which relates to any one certain time, but that we are to use it over a lifetime, according to Paul's teaching in Romans 6. "We are buried with him by baptism into death."

Baptism of Infants

It is agreed that the Baptism of infants is approved by the ancient authors of the church. Origen and Augustine write that it was received from the apostles. And Cyprian, Chrysostom, and Augustine, arguing against Julian, likewise clearly demonstrate this with respect to the merits of sinners. I have wanted this to be said beforehand, since it is profitable to know what the ancients thought about so great an issue. We must not differ with them without certain and clear testimonies of Scripture.

At this particular time some are disapproving of infant Baptism and are demanding that adults be baptized again. Although these dogmas have no firm witnesses from the Scriptures, nevertheless some have embraced them. The authors of this error have spread abroad many other dogmas about community property and the abolition of magistrates. Moreover, since these fanatical spirits parade before them such signs and marks of impiety, it ought to be justly suspected that they are guilty of novelty in other dogmas. Christ has foretold about the last times that it would happen that many would be seduced. Therefore we ought to be more vigilant in this respect and receive no dogma without certain and clear Scriptures.

Now to the cause which I defend. This much is agreed, that the promise of grace and of the kingdom of God relates also to infants. Of this opinion we have clear evidence in the Scriptures. In the first place, it has been commanded that even infants should be circumcised. Circumcision was a sign of promised grace and of promised seed, in which all peoples were to be blessed. Paul in Romans 4 calls circumcision a sign of righteousness. And in Genesis 17 it is written: "I will be their God." Likewise: "The male whose foreskin has not been circumcised shall have his life destroyed from his people." What else are these sentences but promises of grace? For when he says, "I will be their God," he signifies that he wishes to have mercy on them and to preserve them. And subsequently, when he threatens those who are not circumcised, he certainly witnesses that he receives into grace those who have been circumcised while those who have not been circumcised he does not receive. By this we know that circumcision is to be considered as a true and certain sign of grace.

I am not yet speaking of Baptism. I am only deducing this, that the promise of grace and of life eternal pertains to infants also. And that is true, for if circumcision, which is the sign of grace, pertains to infants, it necessarily follows that grace and remission of sins also pertain to infants. In the second place, in Matthew 19 it is written: "Suffer little children to come unto me and forbid them not, for of such is the kingdom of heaven." Some get around this sentence in this manner: Christ is not here saying that the kingdom of heaven is of little children but of those who are like little children. But this interpretation is refuted by the preceding words. For Christ orders little ones to be brought to him. Wherefore grace must pertain to them also, otherwise they would not have been brought to Christ but would have been cast away among the enemies of God. Likewise, even if we are not to interpret Christ's words especially in relation to little children, but as applying to those who are like them, it nevertheless appears that he approves and receives little children, for otherwise he would not approve those who have become like them.

Lastly, Mark says: "He blessed them . . . ," which cannot be accepted in any other sense than that he received them into grace and that he commended them to the Father to be sanctified and blessed, etc. For this purpose examples indeed must be brought forth. For there is no doubt but that the kingdom of God pertains to those male infants who were slaughtered by Herod, as the evangelist signifies when he quotes a passage in Jeremiah about the holy martyrs. And thus, since we have settled this fact that the kingdom of God pertains even to infants, it should now be seen to what infants it relates. For if it pertains to all infants, even those outside the church, there is no need for them to be baptized. But if there is no remission of sins except where the Word and the Sacraments are, the remission of sins will relate to those to whom either Word or Sacrament is applied.

But no testimony can be brought forth from the Scriptures to the effect that the promise of grace pertains to little children who are outside the church. But it is confessed that there is no remission of sins where neither Word nor Sacraments appear, as Peter says in Acts 4: "For there is no other name under heaven given to men whereby we must be saved." Accordingly, since the remission of sins is only there where there is either Word or Sacraments, it follows that salvation pertains to those infants to whom the Sacrament is applied, which is a sign and a testimony of grace promised for all ages and not only for adults.

I see that no firm reasoning, no clear testimony of Scripture can be posited against this reasoning. Since the remission of sins is only there where the Word and the Sacrament are, it follows that the remission of sins pertains to those infants who are attached to the church and to whom the sign of promised grace is applied. But if this reasoning does not seem sufficiently strong to our opponents, let them show and prove themselves that the remission of sins pertains to infants who are outside of the church, unless, of course, they prefer to think that the promise of grace does not at all pertain to infants. Above we have shown the opposite. But they say: "Baptism requires the Word and faith; but since infants do not understand, they have neither the Word nor faith." Against this reasoning of our opponents, we bring up the example of circumcision which, although it required the Word for faith, was nevertheless applied to infants by divine command. But circumcision and Baptism are obviously signs of the same grace of Christ. For circumcision was a sign not only of a corporal promise, but rather of a promised seed, namely, Christ, as Paul also attests in Romans 4, when he calls it a sign of righteousness. And in Galatians he teaches that the promise of grace and of righteousness was before the law.

Therefore, just as circumcision witnessed at that time that the remission of sins pertained to infants, although they did not yet employ reason and could not yet understand the Word, so also now Baptism attests to the fact that the remission of sins relates to infants even if they do not yet understand the preaching of the Word.

But if our opponents strongly contend that infants understand nothing, in the same manner they will be able to conclude either that all infants belong to the kingdom of God or else none at all do. Since this is absurd, let them confess that the remission of sins pertains to those infants to whom the Sacrament is applied. But no command, they say, forces us to baptize infants. To this I reply that although we do not have any express command, nevertheless we do have an example which ought to be valid when Scripture has not ordered otherwise.

And so we do have reasons taken from Scripture. Therefore let our opponents first show where Scripture actually forbids us to baptize infants. Then let them show why it is not permissible for the example of circumcision to be transferred to Baptism, since both signs signify the same Christ. Lastly, let them refute this reason of ours that is taken from Scripture, namely, that since the promise of grace relates to infants and there is no remission of sins outside the church, it follows that to infants must be applied the sign which witnesses that the remission of sins relates to them. Although this reason is taken from Scripture, our opponents falsely accuse us of approving the Baptism of infants without the authority of Scripture. So you see how unsafe it is to agree with those who forbid the baptizing of little children. It has nowhere been written or represented that the remission of sins is there where there is neither Word nor Sacrament. Therefore the Catabaptists will never be able to affirm that those infants to whom Baptism is not applied are saved or attain to the remission of sins. What witness of Scripture, what example, what reason from Scripture would they give that we may know that infants outside of the church attain to the remission of sins?

From this it can be understood how uncertain are the things which our opponents are teaching and this one thing could take away credence from the Catabaptists and that is the fact that when they disapprove of baptism of little children they affirm a most uncertain thing, namely, that the remission of sins belongs in some place where there is neither Word nor Sacrament. Therefore, since their dogmas are so uncertain, it is clear how dangerous it is to receive them against the ancient consensus of the church which has most weighty reasons taken from Scripture. But here, incidentally, it must also be said that sin is remitted unto infants. Moreover, I see that it was pleasing to the ancient writers that original sin was remitted unto infants. For so writes Augustine, often in other places, but especially against Julian, and he quotes the evidences of other writers also. This judgment we shall follow. For Baptism must not be accepted as an empty sign, but as a sign of the remission of sins and as a witness of the divine will, as I have said above.

Therefore, at this point we must set forth just how original sin is remitted. Now, Christian authors call original sin a corruption of human nature, in view of the fact that we are born without the knowledge of God, without fear of him and without faith. And furthermore, at birth we have concupiscence, by which we are dragged into openly disgraceful acts. This corruption of human nature followed the curse after Adam's fall. However, at this time there are some who, while philosophizing too much, deny that this corruption is sin, but they disagree entirely with Scripture. Augustine marvels that during his day there were those who denied original sin, since there was no man in the church previously who thought thus. He says: "From the very beginning right up to the present time in which this novelty has appeared, this doctrine in the faith of the church about original sin has been safeguarded with so great constancy . . ." Even more than this, in our times the shrewdness of certain ones who laugh at the ancient dogma of original sin must be censured. But we shall collect passages from the Scriptures which teach both that human nature has been corrupted and that this corruption is truly sin. Romans 5: "By one man sin entered into the world and then death came upon all men, for all have sinned." And Ephesians 2: "We were by nature children of wrath even as others also." But to be children of wrath is to possess sin of such a nature as that at which God is enraged and which he condemns. And, moreover, it is written in the Psalm: "For behold I was shapen in iniquity and in sin did my mother conceive me," that is, when I was formed, I was unclean and I contracted sin. And Genesis 8: "The design of the human heart is evil from the beginning."

Now this signifies that we are not corrupted by imitation or by the examples of the wicked, as the Pelagians thought and the philosophers judge. But the nature of the human heart within itself, from the very beginning, carries concupiscence, as if to say that concupiscence exists in our nature, before the thought of imitation. And I by no means know whether the word "design" here must be taken with respect to nativity and the design of the foetus. Here belongs that passage from John 1: "Who are born not of blood." For the Evangelist condemns all who have not been "born of God." And John 3 states: "That which is born of the flesh is flesh." Romans 8 also: "The flesh cannot be subject to the law of God." But it could be subject to the law of God if at birth it did not carry along with itself corruption and sin. Therefore we ought to think that human nature is corrupt, that is, we are born without fear of God and without confidence toward God. Likewise we ought to think that when we are born we bring concupiscence along with us, which, as Paul says, is working in our members, producing vices. Further, let us hold that this corruption is sin of such a nature that God condemns it. Philosophers have wondered what is the reason why men are carried off with such force into vices and are unable to submit to reason, although it admonishes right things. But Christian doctrine teaches us that original sin is the reason, since after the sin of Adam his posterity has been cursed. And from this stems that corruption of human nature. For as a tree is barren if God curses it, so has human nature been corrupted and weakened after we became children of wrath.

Now I return to the institution. Original sin is forgiven infants, not in such a way as a total sickness is immediately healed, but it is forgiven them in such a way that they are not considered guilty of that sin, or as the ancients say, as long as we live in this flesh, the residue of the sickness remains but its guilt is destroyed. For children are received into grace and are sanctified by God. For just as it was written of circumcision: "I will be their God . . . ," that is, I will receive them into grace and will protect, sanctify, and direct them; in such manner also these children who have been commended unto God are received into grace, sanctified, and protected by God.

For although they do not yet employ reason, nevertheless God impels them in a way of their own. For neither does reason work Christian righteousness in old men, but God inspires them with true fear and reveals sin to those whom he has called unto repentance and through faith arouses them again and justifies them. The Holy Spirit brought it about that John, though not yet born, felt the presence of Christ. In such a manner other elect infants also can be sanctified by the Holy Spirit, without the aid of reason.

Thus far I have spoken about infant Baptism. Augustine said that we should the more strongly contend in their behalf because they cannot speak for themselves! Moreover, this is the sum of my reasoning. Since there is no remission of sins where there is neither Word nor Sacrament, it follows that the remission of sins relates to those infants to whom the Sacrament is applied, which claims to relate to the remission of sins. And if anyone should contend that the Sacrament must not be administered to those who do not understand the Word, or that the Sacrament alone does not signify the remission of sins, then let him be opposed with the example of circumcision which signified that grace pertained to infants, although they had not yet understood the Word. And this example demonstrates that the use of the Sacrament alone belongs among those who do not understand the Word.

If anyone should ask what Baptism confers upon children, this is my reply: It signifies that the promise of grace pertains to them. However, since there is no remission of sins where there is neither Word nor Sacrament, it follows that those secure the remission of sins to whom the Sacrament is applied. For the whole church believes that the remission of sins is in that place where the Word and the sign are. And, bearing this faith before her, she commends infants unto God, since Christ says: "Suffer the little children to come unto me." And he adds the sign because it is not certain that the remission of sins is in any place where there is no Word or sign. There is no reason at all why the Catabaptists should disapprove of this faith of the church, for they will never be able to show that there is any remission of sins outside the church. Those who demand that we be baptized again follow this one reason, that it is not lawful to baptize children. But Scripture does not forbid their Baptism, and Christ has testified that they are suitable for the kingdom of God. For he orders them to be brought to him, and he says that of such is the kingdom of heaven. He signifies that they have been given guardian angels by the Father, for thus he speaks: "Their angels in heaven always behold the face of my Father in heaven." Without a doubt, those are children of God who are guarded by the angels. Since this is so, why do those fellows exclude them from the church and from the Sacraments, since it is not established that there is remission of sins where there is neither Word nor Sacrament? Therefore, since there is no reason why infant Baptism should be disapproved, there is no necessity for us to be baptized again. But those who demand that we be baptized again think that Baptism is a work of some certain period, namely, when you have begun to repent and believe, then it is they order us to use Baptism, that the sign may agree with the spirit. What will they do? Will they baptize as often as they repent, after having lapsed into sin? But these persons do not seem to me to understand sufficiently either the function of a sign or the nature of repentance, while at the same time they think that signs are applied to bear witness of our faith before men.

But we have taught above that signs are not only evidences of our faith toward men but they have been handed down to be evidences of the divine will toward us, just like the Word itself. Therefore, just as at one place indoctrination precedes justification, so even at another place Baptism should precede repentance; nevertheless, it must not on that account be condemned. Some persons learn many things before they arrive at justification. Is, therefore, the Word which they have learned false or must it be cast out of their mind? Accordingly, neither should Baptism, even if it has been applied before time, on that account be washed away, for the Word by no means has less dignity than the sign. Moreover, as the Word which you have once learned subsequently also arouses and confirms your hearts, so also Baptism, once it has been applied, arouses you throughout a lifetime to repentance and faith. Therefore, Baptism pertains not to any one certain period, just as repentance is not of any one period, for the flesh should be mortified throughout all of life and carnal security should be put off, and, on the other hand, faith and spiritual peace of heart ought to grow.

From these facts it can be concluded that those baptized in infancy should not be baptized over again. See, moreover, how the doctrine of the Catabaptists has no usefulness. They wrangle very much about the ceremony itself, but there is a great silence about the use of the sign. Let us consider rather the use and contemplate the words of Baptism, which can marvelously raise up and confirm terrified consciences. For to what do those words relate: "to be baptized in the name of the Father, and of the Son, and of the Holy Spirit"? They testify that the Father and the Son, and the Holy Spirit receive us and in such a manner that, although we know that we have deserved eternal wrath, although we are dying, yet they are present with us, they forgive our sins, and they want to give us new life.

Thus God makes a covenant with us both through sign and Word, because he has had mercy upon us, and in this dipping he wishes to sprinkle us with the blood of his Son. And having mortified our flesh, he wishes to effect in us spiritual life. When, therefore, the prostrate conscience has been terrified as much as possible and thinks that it deserves nothing but death and wrath, then let it look at this spectacle and think that it has truly been immersed in water and let it know that the Father and the Son and the Holy Spirit are present and wish to pardon and to preserve.

For precisely in order that the remission of sins might be believed, they have ordered us to be baptized in his name. They have commanded his name to be made known to us in order that we might call upon him and believe the divine promises. The form of speech, "in the name of the Father and of the Son, etc.," you can understand in the same sense in which it is used in the Psalms: "Some trust in chariots and some in horses, but we in the name of the Lord," that is, we fight at the command of God and because of this we are supported by his presence and help. Thus we are baptized in the name of the Father and of the Son and of the Holy Spirit. Since we are baptized by his order and ordinance, we ought to feel that he has received us into his grace, that he is present, that he aids us, and that he will save us. The situation amounts to the same thing if you would interpret "in the name of" (in nomine) by the words 'in the place of" (vice), because he who baptizes "in the place of" God signifies that God himself baptizes. Therefore, if the Father himself immerses us into death and sprinkles us with the blood of his Son and sanctifies us through the Holy Spirit, he will without any doubt make us alive. Nor will the sentence be otherwise if you read "into the name of the Father" so as to signify that we have already been made the property of God, and having been reconciled unto God, we can call upon the name of the Lord God and know that we are his care and are saved by him and freely justified.

These words of Baptism must be regarded as the means to stir up faith, and in them we may see just how the divine goodness pours itself out upon us and reveals itself to us that we may believe and be saved. Accordingly, let us pray God to stir up and to promote faith in us so that we can discern and proclaim so great a force of goodness. And this exercise of faith, to use the words of Christ, is among the weightier matters of the Law, but ceremony itself is in another class. We have shown as much as we could at this time just how foolish is the dogma of the Anabaptists, for it is indeed permissible to baptize infants also since to them relates the remission of sins, which does not exist where there is neither Word nor Sacrament. And just as the Baptism of anyone who has been baptized before is not to be rejected on that account, so the Word that you learn before justification must not be unlearned or rejected.

Moreover, the Anabaptists have many other marks by which they declare by what spirit they are being led. Paul orders us to try the spirits. And thus they counsel evil with themselves who join with this faction before they have become thoroughly acquainted with and have comprehended the nature of the whole matter. What they teach is simply ungodly: that it is not permissible for Christians to administer civil offices or to obey the decisions of magistrates, to execute judgments, or to use the sword against criminals, and similar teachings concerning which topics we have often spoken in other places.

And this dogma also is ungodly, that they demand that Christians have all their property in common. Concerning this matter we shall now speak in passing. For indeed that dogma of community property is one of the firebrands of sedition which these fanatics are scattering among the masses. I think that those must be regarded as seditionists who reject the publicly received laws about the distribution of property, no less than those who deny entirely that it is right for a Christian to hold a civil office.

Therefore I conclude that it is permitted unto Christians to hold their own property or to possess riches. Paul confirms this opinion in 2 Corinthians 9, where he teaches that one must distribute as much as he wishes, not sorrowfully or by force; here he clearly teaches that Christians are not to be compelled to forsake their property. But if it were a sin to be rich, no doubt he would demand and order them to flee from riches and he would not leave it up to the judgment of each person to distribute as much as he wills.

And to Timothy he says: "Charge the rich that they be not haughty nor trust in uncertain riches . . ." He does not charge them to depart from their possessions nor to collect their treasures in common. And if it is a sin to be rich, why does he count them as being among the Christians? For it would have been fitting that the possession of property be denounced beforehand if the doctrine of Christ demanded it. In Matthew 19 Christ does not say that it is impossible for a rich man to enter into the kingdom of heaven, but that it is difficult. Finally, just as the Gospel approves of the magistracy and other civil ordinances, so also does it approve of buying, selling, and the legal distribution of property. This is what Paul means when he says: "Purchasing just as if you do not possess." It is permissible to buy, to increase possessions, but without greed and avarice. And what follows pertains to similar events of this civil life: "using the world as not abusing it," that is, administer civil offices, contract marriages, work, some of you pursue one art, others another, teach your children, provide food for them, but do all of these things with the fear of God and with faith. Moreover, the rule which Solomon hands down should be followed in the art of household management: "Drink water from thine own cisterns and drink running waters from thine own well. Let thy fountains be dispersed abroad and rivers of water flow in the streets. Be thou alone master of these things, and not strangers with thee. For thy fountains will be blessed."

Moreover this is the meaning of that command: Each man ought to be master of his own fountain, that is, he ought to hold on to his own possessions and lands. But from them rivers of waters are to be led out of doors, that is, we are to distribute to the needy just as much as our practices allow. And, finally, a promise has been added, for it is promised that God will bless the property of those who administer them in that fashion. Thus Scripture demands the duties of charity, not to disturb civil ordinances about the distribution of property or other things, but to preserve them.

But perhaps that passage in the Gospel which reads as follows is brought up: "If thou wilt be perfect, go sell what thou hast and give to the poor and thou shalt have treasures in heaven, and come and follow me." We shall interpret this passage lightly lest the issue become more obscure by a long argument. The command is a personal one, that is, one that pertained properly to that individual person and not to all. For the word is added: "Come thou and follow me." These words prove that Christ has summoned that one who has been called to the office of teaching. And just as he does not summon all to the office of teaching, he does not order all persons to sell their property. This is the simplest interpretation, according to my way of thinking. For circumstances also prove that a general command is not given, but that the rashness of that young man is being castigated by this special manner of the call. For when he gloried that he had kept all the commandments, Christ indicated that he had not even kept the first one, which commands us to love God with our whole heart. But that young man so loves his possessions that, because of them, he is reluctant to take up the ministry of the Word. And since Christ wished to show him that he preferred his riches to God, he ordered him to give away those riches for the sake of God. Besides, this passage orders that wealth be distributed and not that we flee from wealth and possess it in common. For even if he had sold his possessions, nevertheless the money would have remained in his own house rather than being deposited in a common treasury. Augustine was asked somewhere: Should Christians be permitted to keep their riches? For not merely once have dissensions over this matter arisen in the church. Augustine interprets this passage as follows: He feels that there is a certain perfection in fleeing from riches just as virginity also is a certain perfection. Or just as the gift of tongues is a certain perfection, he maintains that the saying "if thou wilt be perfect" must be kept in this statement of Christ. But it is possible to be Christians without this perfection just as without the gift of tongues. For true Christian perfection is not to be located in any external matter such as in riches or in poverty, in marriage or in some other kind of life, but in fear, faith, hope, and in perfect love.

The example of the apostles, who had all things in common, is also brought up. To this I reply that we are disputing about a command, whether it is commanded that we abandon our possessions. Perhaps somewhere among a few such a plan of community property can exist. For example, in the early church it took place among those Christians who were forced to this because the property of those who were proved to have become Christians was being seized. So in order not to have it become the booty of tyrants, they themselves divided their property beforehand. But their example does not impose on others the necessity to do this, just as it does not follow that celibacy must be decreed for the ministers of the church because Paul lived a celibate life.

So community property is not a matter of necessity, but a matter of freedom among a few who have their property in common voluntarily. Ananias was killed because he lied, not because he had withheld his money. For Peter clearly says that the money would have been in his own power. And he said he was angry because Ananias had lied, not to men but to the Holy Spirit, etc.

This argument also is brought up: "Give to everyone that asketh . . ." But it can easily be understood that this sentence does not demand that we give up our property or possessions. For when he commands us to give, he certainly permits us to retain possessions from which we may take that we may then distribute. In 2 Corinthians 8 Paul interprets this passage to mean that we must so give lest "some be released and ye be burdened." Accordingly, this passage is to be accepted in the sense that we should distribute, not paltry alms but abundant. They do violence to this passage who distort it in such a way as to make it relate to any such things as community property, by which the ordinance concerning the distribution of property is disturbed. But just as those who take up arms against civil offices are guilty of sedition, so it is sedition to abolish those ordinances which order each and every person to possess his own and to keep away from that of another. The dream of Socrates, who pleasantly jokes about community property in that ideal republic of his, in no way relates to us. For Christ teaches us not to disturb the legitimate ordinances of the states. Nevertheless, in the meantime let us generously help the needy and especially the ministers of the churches and the teachers. For we are especially in debt to them as Scripture often teaches. For never before in the churches have priests been more ungenerously treated than at this time.

Some who are strongly evangelical seize the possessions that have been given for the needs of the church and for studies, without which the teaching of religion cannot be preserved. And the masses everywhere are defrauding their pastors. This is done especially by those who pride themselves on being evangelicals, while the teachers of the Gospel are nowhere being treated more inhumanly. Paul writes that they are worthy of a twofold honor, for which reason all of the offices of love should be especially exercised toward them.

Therefore, let us think thus: Christians do right if, according to the legal ordinance of states, they remain in control of their possessions, provided that each one, in accordance with his means, gives liberally to the needy. A reward for such duties is set forth in the Psalm: "He who distributes and who gives to the poor, his righteousness remains forever." I wanted to warn about this in passing, because I have discovered that among the wicked dogmas of the Anabaptists is this one also: "Christians ought to flee from their possessions and possess them in common." Moreover, it is clear enough that those who teach such wicked dogmas are not of God. There never has been a more perilous time, and we must be the more diligent, lest we accept spirits that have not been tried.

Although Melanchthon deplored very much the doctrinal division between Zwingli and Luther, nevertheless he rejected decisively the standpoint of the Swiss Reformer. He was aroused over the doctrine of Luther and, according to a letter written to Camerarius on October 13, 1528,[1] he was somewhat provoked. Because of his preoccupation with the Saxon visitation from the autumn of 1528 to the end of January 1529, he could not address himself to this question.[2]

During a session of the Speyer Reichstag Oecolampadius wrote to Melanchthon concerning the whole problem and the latter, being deeply influenced by the political situation, was ready to entrust everything to God.[3] He regretted very much the increasing sharpness in the internal Protestant explanation of the issue and felt that a false statement of the question was to be blamed for all of the misunderstanding.

Although he had remained aloof from the controversy over the Lord's Supper, Melanchthon felt it necessary to enter the battle by releasing an open letter. Political figures, like the Landgrave Philip of Hesse, impressed him with the necessity of intervening in order that the theological opposition between Zurich and Wittenberg might be overcome as speedily as possible. At first a colloquy for union commended itself to Melanchthon, but later he had other thoughts on the matter.[4] Then he became conscious of the fact that the division could not be denied. The religious question could not be mixed with political issues, and truth could not be sacrificed to politics.

CHAPTER TEN

LETTER ON THE LORD'S SUPPER

1529

Philip Melanchthon to His Friend, the Most Learned Doctor John Oecolampadius.

I am in receipt of several letters from you which were most gratifying to me, since in them are many clear indications of your long-standing benevolence toward me and of your most constant goodwill. For my attitude toward you is the same as it has always been. Moreover, being animated by an admiration for your learning and your virtues, I have always both loved you very much and respected you because of your outstanding piety. Would that these were times when we could enjoy this great friendship of ours! But now a terrible dissension over the Lord's Supper has arisen, which has somewhat interrupted our long-standing custom of performing the obligations of friendship in which we used to engage mutually. But it has not shaken my goodwill toward you. And so, if you find me lacking in any obligation toward you, I should like you to blame the times rather than my unfaithfulness.

In regard to the cause in which you are now engaged, I am very sorry that a dissension has arisen with respect to the very thing which was instituted by Christ to strengthen mutual love in Christians. Moreover, you know that I have up to this moment stood out as a mere spectator of this drama, rather than as an actor in it. I have many weighty reasons why I have not involved myself in such an odious struggle. Meanwhile, no other concern for any other issue has vexed my very soul more than my concern over this affair. Not only have I myself thought about what can be said on both sides, but I have also sought out the opinions of the ancients on this matter. For I would not want to stand forth either as the author or the defender of any new dogma in the church. Since I have weighed everything which seems to be strongest on both sides, I shall speak with your permission, but in so doing it will not be in defense of your view. For I can discover no firm reason to satisfy a conscience which forsakes the proper significance of words. Moreover, I have written nothing about this affair up to this very day, because I saw that whatever I might write, the unjust critics would say that I had been commissioned by Luther to serve as some sort of household witness. There would be no authority in my judgment, since it would seem to have been written to please another. But I hope you judge better of my character. "Him do I hate even as the gates of hell who says one thing while thinking another in his heart."[5]

Whatever sort of person I am, certainly I have never loved those Epicureans, of whom there are very many at this time, who laugh at religion and take pleasure in deceiving people concerning important matters. As you know, I have always been zealous of Christian doctrine. For this reason it has been my chief concern to learn it diligently. While seeking what I can safely pursue, it is not without small difficulty that I have refrained from scholastic disputations and partly even from the quarrels of my friends; of this matter there are some testimonials extant. But if I were striving after favor —for I am not ignorant of how many great and learned men your faction has on its side—I would not despise their friendship. Accordingly, if your view of the Lord's Supper were pleasing to me, I would simply acknowledge it.

You are contending that the body of the absent Christ is represented as though in a tragedy. But I see standing forth the promises of Christ: "I will be with you even to the consummation of the age," and similar ones, where there is no need to separate divinity from humanity. Therefore I feel that this Sacrament is a witness to the Real Presence. Since this is so, I feel that in the Supper there is a communion of the present body. Since the proper significance of the word does not disagree with any article of faith, there is no sufficient reason why we should give it up. And this view of the presence of the body is in agreement with other writings which speak of the Real Presence of Christ within us. For it is an opinion unworthy of Christians that Christ has so occupied a certain place in heaven that he sits there as though incarcerated. You gather up many absurd arguments which you think support this view. You marshal even some statements of the ancients which seem to favor your case. But these absurd arguments will be less offensive to him who remembers that a judgment about heavenly things must be made in accordance with the Word of God, and not geometry, and who has learned through being tempted that there is no reasoning which can instruct a conscience satisfactorily when it has abandoned the Word of God.

In these topics which you cite from the ancients I recognize that there is a certain difference. Nevertheless, if anyone prudently selects the sayings of the most important of those authors, he will discover very many which indicate that the view which we hold was the common view of the ancient church, insofar as that is known to us. Notwithstanding, you, as a sagacious man, too shrewdly interpret certain passages and distort them to your own cause. When the ancients dispute about the resurrection, they adduce the Supper as an argument, and in my opinion wisely so. Because he instituted the communion of his body Christ indicated to the apostles that he would rise again. For it was necessary that the body which was to be imparted to us should be alive. If the ancients had felt that the absent body was represented, how could they prove the resurrection from this? Even if Christ had not risen, could the absent and destroyed body neverthless be represented, just as Hector is represented in the fables?

I have not now undertaken any disputation, and I have written only these things that you might know my perpetual goodwill toward you. Nevertheless, I have not wanted to conceal what I feel in the matter. I beg you to consider both how grave and dangerous a matter you have undertaken.

This much is true, that truth is lost by too much wrangling. And it is all the more imperiled by such violent controversies as these. Wherefore it would be more fitting for several good men to come together for a colloquy about this matter. I see what seeds for such disputations are scattered throughout the books of the ancients. There are some also in certain works only recently produced, before this present tumult. I see that your cause abounds with the assistance of ingenious persons and that you hold the interest of spectators, not only open but likewise secret. I by no means know if the latter more powerfully support you than those who are in the open. Your modesty is sufficiently known to me, so that I did not consider it necessary for me to admonish you to reflect that even ingenious and wise men sometimes can fall into error and that confidence in one's innate ability is especially dangerous in spiritual matters.

You know that it is written: "Whatever is lofty in this world is an abomination before God." And there are many more persons than it is thought who embrace only those things in religion which they have been able to elicit and understand by their own natural powers. Finally, I beg you to consider this letter of mine favorably, for it is written to an excellent and most friendly spirit. Farewell.

Speyer, 1529.

The Leipzig Colloquy of 1539 and the deliberations with those who had been sent from England forced Melanchthon to occupy himself more deeply with the problem of the church. He delivered a lecture on it in Wittenberg and then prepared a book for his students dealing with the problem.[1] In a letter to Canterbury he gave the outline of the book.

The Frankfurt deliberations of 1539 strengthened Melanchthon in the view that he should call special attention to the agreement of the evangelical church with the ancient church. As he later wrote to Brenz, he still held that view, marking out a mediating position, which he thought was a middle-of-the-road position or a golden mean.[2] He regarded this writing as so important that he gave himself over to it almost entirely in the midst of his other works and missions.[3] On June 24, 1539, he gave this document to Duke Albrecht, to whom he had dedicated it and it found its way to the press.[4] As he wrote to Friedrich Myconius, he was at once conscious of the fact that much improvement had to be made on this book. He asked Myconius for his opinion in order that he might know how to improve the second edition. From the same letter we learn than Melanchthon had the idea of adding a supplement to this little book. But the supplement was not ready on the completion of the work "De Ecclesia," so the manuscript was sent to the press on August 31, 1539.[5] The Latin text translated on the following pages is based on the Wittenberg edition of 1539 according to the copy in the National and City Library at Düsseldorf.

CHAPTER ELEVEN

THE CHURCH AND
THE AUTHORITY OF THE WORD
1539

**To the Most Illustrious Prince and Lord, Lord Albert,
Duke of Prussia, Marquis of Brandenburg, etc.**

Astyages, king of the Medes, enraged at Prince Harpagus because he had not killed the infant Cyrus as he had been ordered, subsequently summoned the young son of Harpagus, and, having slaughtered him, set him before his father to eat at a banquet. The wretched father reclined at the table with the thought that he had been invited to the banquet by the king as a guest of honor and proceeded to chew up the roasted entrails of his son. After dinner, when the tyrant had indulged in many jokes, he finally revealed his cruelty by ordering the head, hands, and feet of the young lad to be brought in. When Harpagus had recognized the limbs of his son, the king asked him whether the feast had pleased him. At that point, although seized with tremendous grief, he nevertheless suppressed it in the presence of the king and placidly replied: "Whatever the king does is indeed pleasing to me."

For many centuries now this type of tyranny has been carried on by the pontiffs and their satellites. They demand that the people without any discrimination approve all of their decrees, even those which are plainly impious, all of their abuses, all of their monkish absurdities, and that they regard them as oracles from heaven.

Now although the authority of the ancients is not to be rashly destroyed, yet, since it is necessary to hold fast to the sure and firm testimonies which have been divinely set forth concerning the will of God and his true worship, this barbaric servitude is by no means to be tolerated in the church. It forbids us to distinguish between true doctrine and that which has been adulterated, and it confirms nefarious abuses. Tyranny is injurious to human nature but much more injurious to the church, in which all of the pious ought to serve as guards and be at their post in order that neither those who superintend nor any others may cover over the Gospel with wicked opinions.

Furthermore, how many vices have spread throughout the church without any definite authors! Indeed, they have arisen first from obscure examples and by degrees have gained great strength. Among these are: praying to saints, the manifold profanation of the mystery of the Lord's Supper, trafficking in masses, the impurities of celibacy, and many other things.

Although these things have stolen in without any decrees of the synods and without any weighty authority, while those in charge of the church slept, nevertheless they are now defended by the harshest penalties and the pretext for such cruelty is zeal for retaining the authority of the church. And many who are equipped with learning and eloquence, although they see that war is being waged against God and although they confess that the glory of God is being polluted, that pious doctrine is being destroyed, and that the members of Christ are being torn apart, nevertheless they applaud the tyrants, even more impudently than did Harpagus. They declare that whatever the pious princes and pontiffs, those fighters against God, murderers, and poor wretches, are doing, is pleasing to them.

Then they skillfully apologize for such deep infamy as this and they imagine that it is beneficial that the authority and the prestige of those who are in charge be preserved. Tyrannies are retained by crime and cruelty as long as they endure, but the authority of the church is not. It is a thing most unworthy, however, especially for learned men, to be like satellites of tyrants and indeed of those who are warring against God, to confirm their fury and inflame their savagery. What more disgraceful thing can be thought of than this bondage, especially among those who are elevated because of their learning to be counselors of kings and rulers of the church, in order that they might be teachers and guardians of true religion and not that they might be flattered by the unjust carnal desires of rulers? But no doubt the situation is just as it says in the tragedy: An evil minister of the palace is the shame of the kingdom.

Those who attach themselves to tyrants and yield to them both thought and tongue cannot look upon their own face without impudence.

Moreover, since the name of the church and of antiquity is given as a pretex for such crimes, I have collected some things about the church and the ancient synods and writers which I hope will be of some value for younger persons to decide when the testimonies of antiquity are valid. The name of the church ought to be as dear to all the pious as the name of their true fatherland. And what is more revered than that venerable council in which the Son of God, our Lord Jesus Christ, presides and holds joined to him a great crowd of the most outstanding persons from the very beginning of the world, such as: Adam, Enoch, Noah, Shem, Abraham, Isaac, Jacob, Joseph, Moses, Samuel, David, Elijah, Elisha, Isaiah, Ezekiel, Daniel, the apostles, and many pious souls whom God has adorned with admirable glory in teaching, and in ruling empires, and upon whose doctrine Christ has bestowed clear witness. It is fitting that we especially venerate such an honorable assembly upon which certain adversaries inflict the highest contumely when they bind it in fetters in order to establish idolatry, confirm prodigious errors, and rationalize murders and infinite cruelty.

Although this book is smaller and briefer than the fullness of the argument demanded, nevertheless I have brought it forth to be published and I have hoped that it would go forth under more favorable auspices if it were to be dedicated to Your Highness, since the name of Your Highness is deservedly most dear to many good and learned men in all Germany because of your excellent virtue, piety, and wisdom. Indeed, there can be no human condition more pleasing to a good and wise prince than if he is praised by the true judgments of good people and is loved by them.

May it be well with you, Your Highness. 1539.

It is a very frequent custom to contend as to just how much weight is to be attributed to the opinions of the church, the decrees of the synods, and the sayings of the Scriptures. For although we do indeed embrace the Word of God, nevertheless, since there seem to be ambiguous passages in apostolic writings, some contend that the opinions of the church are to be followed rather than the writings of the apostles.

Then they add the false claim that the authority of the church is to be preferred to the Word of God and that the church can alter things which have been handed down in the Word of God. As proof for these opinions they quote a passage of Augustine: "I would not believe the Gospel unless the authority of the church moved me to it." Accordingly, under the false pretext of the name of the church, the pontiffs decide and teach in accordance with their own desire many things contrary to the Word of God and confirm and establish false doctrine and false practices. And it is solely the name of the church that is keeping very many persons even now from the true doctrine of the Gospel which we profess. Therefore it is necessary to warn people in a correct manner about the authority of the church.

On the other hand, there are some rather impudent characters who, when weaving new opinions from scriptural sayings which have been grossly distorted, absolutely reject the unanimity of the true church and all of the synods without discrimination. An example is Servetus when he opposes the church of all ages, perverts the statements about the Word in John 1, and seeks after, as he himself thinks, a more elegant interpretation. Therefore, that such impudence be repressed in some manner by walls, so to speak, is a task for the church, just as the ancient synods and writers adduce the primary testimonies accepted by the apostles and certain authors.

Tertullian, arguing against Praxeas, says that this rule is to be invoked against all heretics: That is true which is prior, but that is false which is later. To be sure, he calls "prior" that which the apostles have surely handed down, for so he himself interprets himself.

Irenaeus, arguing against Florinus, asserts the authority of his predecessors, specifically that of Polycarp, who had heard John the Apostle. For he says that John would have condemned the doctrines of Florinus if he had heard them and would have shunned the place in which those things had been said, as if it were polluted.

Basil mentions his nurse, whose piety he says was especially praiseworthy at that time, and adds that she received the doctrine from Gregory of Neo-Caesarea, who at that time was distinguished for his learning and miracles. He refuted Paul of Samosata and left a short confession of faith, which contains an illustrious testimony of the Trinity. It is extant in Book VII of his *Church History.*

Origen mentions the apostles on the Baptism of infants. He says in his comment on Romans 6 that the church has received the tradition from the apostles that infants are to be baptized. These correctly adduce the authority of the church. Wherefore I shall relate in order what the church is, in what respect it must be heard, and how proved testimonies may be used. Nevertheless, doctrine must be judged according to the Word of God in such a way that the highest authority of the Word of God may remain, according to this statement: "If anyone has taught any other gospel, let him be accursed."

In the first place, when I use the word "church," I do not have in mind pontiffs, bishops, and others who approve their opinions. For these are enemies of the true church, partly Epicureans, partly open idolaters. But I call the church the assembly of true believers who have the Gospel and the Sacraments and who are being sanctified by the Holy Spirit, as the church is described in Ephesians 5 and in John 10: "My sheep hear my voice . . ."

Now, although it is necessary for this true church to last forever, since the kingdom of Christ is perpetual as it is written: "I will be with you even to the end of the age," nevertheless, it must be known that this true church does not always flourish to the same degree, but often is quite small. And from time to time it must be divinely renewed when true teachers have been sent, as in the time of Noah, when the church was small and an assembly of only a few.

Thus after the flood Melchizedek, who was Shem, the son of Noah, retained the true doctrine. And when idolatry grew among the Chaldeans, and the true doctrine was almost everywhere extinct, God renewed the church by calling Abraham. Subsequently the family of Abraham and a few of his hearers were the church. Meanwhile, the Chaldeans and Egyptians were gloating over the fact that they were the descendants of the fathers, and that they were retaining the examples and worship of the fathers. They were declaring that they were the people of God, although they had not retained the Word of God, even if they did retain the ceremonies, to which, however, they had joined perverse opinions and added idolatry.

In the time of Ahab the church was almost extinct, but subsequently it was restored again by Elijah and Elisha, and then it collapsed again.

When Christ was born, the church in Judah was quite small, consisting of Mary, Joseph, the family of Zechariah, Simeon, Anna, the shepherds, and a few others. Meanwhile, ecclesiastical authority was vested in the Pharisees and the Sadducees, who were openly wicked. The Sadducees were even Epicureans, but nevertheless they appropriated unto themselves the special title of the people of God.

In like manner, in the time of the prophets the true church was small, as is stated in Isaiah 1: "Except the Lord had left us seed, we would have become like Sodom and Gomorrah." These words seriously warn us that we should not think of the church as though it were a worldly state and that we should not measure it by the succession of bishops or by the rank and place of pontiffs. But we should hold that the church is to be found among those who retain the true doctrine of the Gospel. In this number there are necessarily some true believers, for the promises pertain to this assembly. Therefore Isaiah takes away that august title from his princes and pontiffs and says that a small seed was left in that very people that was called the people of God.

And in the time of Jeremiah, when the kings and the priests were opposed to him, the church was not the assembly of priests, but those who believed the discourses of Jeremiah. Amos 3 says: "Israel will be liberated just as a shepherd snatches two legs from the throat of a lion." Finally, the church was small in comparison with the multitude of the wicked, since all of the nations outside of the people of Judah had lost entirely the knowledge of God.

Even Scripture declares that after the apostles calamities will come to the church, as we read in Matthew 24: "Many false prophets will arise and draw away many." Likewise: "When you see the abomination of desolation standing in the holy place . . ." This signifies that in the church, which is so called, idolatry will arise by which true doctrine and true worship will be overwhelmed. Destruction will come to the church, that is, solitude or extinction. And so it has happened. After abuses of the masses and the worship of traditions arose, there followed darkness about true worship, about faith, about praying in faith, about the duties of one's calling. For the conscience intent on its own merits cannot understand the remission of sins, nor true prayer and waiting on divine help, etc.

Other references include Matthew 24: "There shall be signs and wonders of such a nature that, if possible, they will deceive the very elect"; 2 Thessalonians 2: "A falling away shall come . . ."; Luke 18: "Do you think that when the Son of Man cometh he shall find faith"; Psalm 89: "Hast thou vainly established all the sons of men . . ." For this is a complaint against the future ruination of the church. These sayings bear witness that although the church of necessity is to be preserved, nevertheless, especially in the last times, it is to be quite small and an assembly of a few who are despised and cast off in this life, just as Paul says: "Not many wise, not many mighty . . ."

I have cited these witnesses here that it might first be considered thoroughly what the church is and that the soul might be led away from those carnal opinions which imagine that the church is a state of pontiffs and which bind it to the regular succession of bishops, just as empires consist of the regular succession of princes. But the church is constituted in another manner. For its assembly is not bound to regular succession, but to the Word of God. The church is born again where God restores the doctrine and confers the Holy Spirit. Paul in Ephesians 4 witnesses that in this manner churches are guided and preserved, and not by ordinary succession. "He has given gifts to men, apostles, prophets, etc." For he teaches that that is truly the church in which Christ is effectual and to which he gives true teachers.

Therefore, when the name and the authority of the church are thrown up to us, let us first consider whether mention is being made of the true church or indeed of the assembly of the pontiffs and of their succession and state. Nor should we allow ourselves to be frightened away from the Word of God by any false pretext of the term "church."

In the second place, after I have said what the true church is, I now must add that this true church, which is small and which consists of the saints only, retains the true doctrine of the Gospel or the articles of faith, just as Paul calls it the seat of truth. But this true church herself possesses the doctrine sometimes more, sometimes less pure and clear. The church has many weak members also. The apostles were the church, but they did not understand before the resurrection of Christ what the nature of Christ's kingdom would be. Peter, even after the Holy Spirit had been given, imagined that the practices of the law were necessary, but, warned from heaven, he taught that the kingdom of Christ was not a Jewish state, but spiritual and perpetual observances (Acts 10).

Later, when the preaching of the apostles had begun, the pure and clear doctrine was shining in them. But in the meantime there were many weak ones who, although they were true members of the church and held the articles of faith, still added some error, such as those who were observing the practices of the law. They did not properly understand true observances and the abrogation of the law. This error was not unimportant and was spreading some

obscurity over the articles of faith. So Christ foretold concerning
the church in the last time that there would be a great darkness
which would hinder even the elect from having pure doctrine.

Therefore some part of the true church remains and it retains the
articles of faith but at times its practices are less pure and obscured
by some detrimental opinions containing some error. Now I am
still speaking of the true members of the church and the saints, not
of others who have lost the light of the Word and who are without the Holy Spirit, and who follow the judgment of reason. Although they think that they transmit quite pious things, they actually speak strange and wicked things. So there are now many who
are outstanding in learning, in good character, and have the appearance of piety, and who seem to themselves to speak the most
holy things, although they are far from the true light, that is, from
a true understanding of the Word of God. To such I have not yet
referred, but up to now mention has been made only of the true
members of the church, who are for the most part weak.

Paul says: "No one can lay another foundation, save that which
is laid. But one builds on it gold, another wood, another straw . . ."
By foundation he understands articles of faith, that is, the sum of
Christian doctrine and the doctrine of Christ's benefits, but to this,
he says, some will add useful doctrine and interpretation and true
spiritual observances. These he calls gold. Others will add straw,
that is, improper opinions and those containing some error, which
was the case also in the beginning when ceremonies, which brought
false opinions along with them, were immediately instituted.

To my way of thinking, Ambrose is a true member of the church.
Nevertheless, he makes the following comment on the Christian
fast of forty days: "Other fasts are voluntary, but this one is by
necessity." Now this opinion is straw that has been added to the
doctrine of faith.

Similarly, Basil added monasticism as so much straw and praises
this type of life with extravagant and false commendations, although
he was indeed reprimanded by his bishop. But that it is not any
small error to institute new observances is the frequent warning
of Scripture, as this one passage sufficiently indicates: "In vain they
worship me with the mandates of man." It is a serious sin against
the First Commandment to institute or approve practices not required by God. For when the First Commandment prohibits "other"
gods, it prohibits "other" (alienos) practices.

Cyprian urges canonical penalties, of which some use was made at that time, and confirms opinions as if they are necessary and as if sins are remitted because of them. Sometimes he says that absolution without them is useless. Perhaps he was thinking better than he spoke. Nevertheless, these errors are not slight but are like very thick straw obscuring the pure doctrine about Christ's benefits, and about faith.

Moreover, writers have often thought more correctly than they speak, since very many have been quite negligent and incorrect in teaching and borrow from the common crowd many opinions and formulas in which there are some errors. So Augustine adopts the term "satisfactions" from the crowd, even though he reproves openly the errors about satisfactions. He misrepresents himself in his interpretation of this opinion. Every sin is voluntary when he is disputing about original sin, but when his opinion is a public saying, it is a tradition about external crimes.

Thus they call the Supper of the Lord an offering, although it was not instituted as an offering. But Christ himself was the Priest, offering up his own sacrifice. Nor was there in times past any offering of the body and blood made in the ceremony of the Supper. Before the consecration, bread and other things were offered up, and the priest used to say that he was offering up prayers, thanksgiving, and the whole service of worship, which is usually done in the Supper. Therefore, although it was in no manner understood as an offering, yet subsequently the name was distorted to that of an offering of the body, whence great abuses have ensued.

Although Dionysius, in the book which contains the ceremonies of the church, carefully described the ceremony of gathering up, he still makes no mention whatsoever of any offering of the Lord's body. Nor does the Canon of Basil contain the word "offering." Later I shall say more about the Lord's Supper. I have included these things only to show that the ancients sometimes borrowed inappropriate expressions from the multitude, as is customarily done in all ages.

Sometimes under the influence of the opinions and examples of the multitude, which is not pious, the ancients were drawn into superstitions created by the human imagination, as in the Synod of Nicea, where, unless one man, Paphnutius, had stood in the way, they would have approved the opinion of those who wanted the decree to be made that priests should abstain from their wives. Custom so bound Cyprian and many others that they approved the prohibition of marriage.

Likewise, the whole Synod of Nicea, bound by the opinion of the multitude or of the time, approved the canons of penance, which subsequently propagated errors, too grievous to be borne. The examples of leaders often deceive even the pious, as did the example of Antony, which spread darkness over many people. So far I have spoken of the pious; although they are saints, nevertheless most of them are weak. I shall add a few words now about the fallen.

Sometimes the pious fall away completely and lose the Holy Spirit; Origen lapsed completely in judgment, especially if he affirmed these prodigious errors: that there have been innumerable worlds; that in the end the devils are to be saved. Tertullian also wickedly condemns second marriages. Perhaps, however, they recovered their senses. For many who have truly fallen away in life and doctrine nevertheless do return to their senses. And it very frequently happens that saints truly fall and do not judge according to the Word and spiritual light, but are deceived by the imagination of reason; nevertheless, they then return to their senses. So it was with Gideon, when he fell away completely by instituting a practice in accordance with human counsel.

From all these things, this conclusion follows: Although the true church, which is small, retains the articles of faith, nevertheless this same true church can possess errors which obscure the articles of faith. Besides, many so lapse that they approve entirely impious errors contrary to the articles of faith, even if some do perhaps return to their senses.

In the first place, therefore, whenever the authority of the church is adduced, one must ascertain whether it has been the consensus of the true church, congruent with the Word of God.

In the second instance, it must be said that writers who are extant often have fallen away, and it is quite possible that some of them are not even members of the church.

In the third place, another distinction must be added, namely, that in that assembly which we call the church there is a large number of irreverent persons, very many of whom excel others in authority, in the appearance of religion, and in doctrinal opinion. Such, for instance, was the case among the people of Judah in Jeremiah's time. I refer to the high priests and other irreverent priests, who were even themselves invoking the promises and the authority of their status and of the law: "The law will not perish from the priests." They denied that their assembly could err, when on the

contrary at that very time they were entirely in error and dis-
agreed with Jeremiah. Likewise, at the time of Christ there were
very few pious ones, for example, Zechariah and Simeon.

Furthermore, whenever an irreverent group rules in the church,
it establishes many false and impious things in the name of the
church. Such a crowd has embraced the rite of applying masses
to the benefit of the living and the dead, the worship of vows and
of saints, and later the precedent has done injury to the pious.
Such a crowd, even in a synod, decreed that the marriages of
priests had to be torn apart. However, it happens often in the
church that the irreverent who excel in ability arrogate to themselves the power of establishing religion by human wisdom. Since
they are not moved by the Word of God but are led on by rational
imagination and search out elegant opinions, they bring forth
wicked dogmas, as did Paul of Samosata, Arius, and Pelagius.
Others are in search of merits or of a splendid authority and regi-
men for the people and by these causes are moved to institute and
pile up observances, as did the monks and Gregory. And at this
particular time the pontiffs, princes, and many learned men, eager
to establish the church, are moved by human wisdom, and having
abandoned the Word of God, wish to constitute the church according to their own imaginations. Nor do they see that it is a terrible
piece of impiety to depart from the Word of God, to seek God
without the Word, to institute practices by human judgment without any mandate from God, to change true dogmas and to suppress
the purity of the Word of God.

Whenever, then, the authority of the church is thrown up to us—
such as about the rite of applying masses to the benefit of others,
or that the church does not err, or that the church has applied
masses for so many centuries and therefore the custom must be
preserved—we must reply all the more emphatically that the universal church, which is the multitude of those ruling in the church,
can err, just as the high priests and other priests did in the time
of Jeremiah or of Christ. And although, in addition to that multitude, there are some pious ones who retain the articles of faith,
nevertheless these also, moved by precedents, give assent to certain errors. Thus it comes about that they retain less pure articles
of faith, as did Bernard, who seems to have thought more correctly
than others, although he assented to many errors, such as the abuse
of the masses, the power of the pope, vows, and the worship of
saints.

Therefore the authority of the multitudes must not be asserted over against the Word of God, but we must return to the rule: "If any person should teach any other gospel, let him be accursed." Let the authority of the Word divinely transmitted be primary. Then that body is to be considered the church which agrees with that Word, as Christ says: "My sheep hear my voice." And Augustine says: "The question is, Where is the church?" What, therefore, are we to do? Are we to seek it in our own words, or in the words of its head, our Lord Jesus Christ? I think that we ought to seek the church in the words of him who is the truth and who best knows his own body.

But here the objection is made: If the authority of the church is repudiated, then too great license is conceded to the haughtiness of ingenious persons, for, having rejected the opinions of the church, many will contrive new and impious interpretations of the Scriptures. Although this danger is not to be taken lightly and although it is good to hold such license in check, it must be considered again to what degree the authority of the church is to be deemed requisite. For when Servetus renews the impious error of Paul of Samosata and denies that the Word is to be understood as a person in that passage which reads: "In the beginning was the Word . . .," he proclaims magnificently the authority of the Scriptures and orders that this is to be preferred to the decrees of the church. Then he disputes shrewdly that language must be understood in a simple way. Moreover, since in common ordinary conversation the term "Word" does not mean a person, he denies that it is to be understood as "person" in John, so that if Demosthenes were to read this passage: "In the beginning was the Word," he certainly would not think some person to be understood.

Therefore I ask whether it is not good to oppose the authority of the church against such persons. To this I respond that just as the Gospel enjoins us to hear the church, so I always say that that assembly within which the Word of God has been honored, and which is called the church, must be heard, as we also order our pastors to be heard. Let us, therefore, hear the church when she teaches and admonishes, but not believe merely because of the authority of the church. For the church does not originate articles of faith; she only teaches and admonishes. But we must believe because of the Word of God when, to be sure, admonished by the church, we understand that a particular opinion has been handed down in the Word of God truly and without sophistry.

Perhaps Demosthenes would not think the reference was to a "person" if he were to read: "In the beginning was the Word." But a hearer, admonished by the church that the term "Word" signifies a person, namely the Son of God, is being assisted by the church as it teaches and admonishes; he believes the article not because of the authority of the church, but because he sees that this opinion has firm proofs in Scripture itself and he sees that the words are being spoken about a certain person who assumed human nature in this world and lived with men. This person, he understands, is called "the Word." He collects appropriate and firm testimonies about the two natures of Christ. For he knows that concerning the nature of God the voice from heaven must be believed and that it is the height of impiety for opinions about the nature of God to be invented without God's own testimony. First Peter 1 and Matthew 17 say: "Hear ye him."

Moreover, the first church is strong as a witness of the apostles. I am speaking, however, about dogmas, not about human traditions. For dogmas the apostles intended to be firm and perpetual. Human rites they did not mean to be perpetual and immutable. Nor did the apostles err in doctrine. Therefore it is good to hold fast to them when the most ancient writers adduce the authority of the apostles.

For instance, Origen, Tertullian, Irenaeus, Gregory of Neo-Caesarea, Bishop Alexander of Alexandria, and many others cite them on the Trinity. Since they witness that the doctrine of the Trinity was received from the apostles, they strongly confirm the faithful. And so such testimonies are not to be spurned.

Moreover, as I have said that the ancient writers are to be heard, so now I also state that the polemicists are to be heard, since some remain in the church who retain the truth, sometimes rather purely, at other times quite impurely. But I must add that when heard, they must be judged according to the Word of God, which abides always as the rule of doctrine.

Examples

Augustine contends more eagerly than the rest about original sin. He teaches, therefore, and admonishes, and when we see him truly and without sophistry reciting the opinion of Scripture, we believe the article, not because of Augustine, but because of the Word of God. And we see that writers before him feel the same way, even if they have not treated this article as fully or as clearly as he.

Other Examples

Peter, Bishop of Alexandria, contends against Meletius that the fallen (Christians) ought to be received again and asserts the authority of the ancients. For Epiphanius relates these words as the doctrine recounts which has come down even to us: The illustrious Bishop of Alexandria teaches, therefore, and admonishes that fallen Christians ought to be received again. This we believe, not because of this bishop, but because we see that this teaching has been handed down in the Word of God and the testimonies of the ancient church agree with it.

I say the same thing about the synods: The synods of the church which, while disputing about the Word of God, do teach and admonish us, are to be heard. But let judgment be used and when they yield us things that are true, let us believe them because of the Word of God. For example, the Synod of Nicea piously and usefully taught and admonished all posterity about the Son of God, but we believe the article, not because of the synod, but because we see it has been so transmitted in the Word of God.

Other things which are outside of the Scriptures are not to be so embraced, such as when the Synod of Nicea instituted the canons of penance, which are human traditions outside of the Scriptures and have been the seeds for a multitude of superstitious opinions.

The guests of Samson would not have been able to interpret the riddle proposed at the feast unless they had interrogated his consort. Whereupon Samson said: "If you had not ploughed with my heifer, you would not have discovered my riddle." Thus we must look around to see where that assembly is which has the Word of God and we must see which assembly of the Fathers and of the synods is purer, that is, which has fewer opinions that are outside of the Word of God. Such things as these the church teaches, admonishes, and witnesses. But we must see whether the things she sets forth have the firm testimonies of the Word of God.

But no doubt it is fitting for the pious to confess that the fathers who have fought in the most bitter controversies and have retained pious dogmas are well deserving of posterity. That benefit is not easy to be deduced. To this pertains the statement of Augustine: "I would not believe the Gospel, except the authority of the church should move me to it." Augustine does not feel that the authority of the church is greater than that of the Word of God, nor does he feel that the church can abolish articles handed down in the Word.

But he feels that the church is a teacher and a witness. We would not believe the Gospel if the church did not teach us and did not witness that this doctrine has been handed down by the apostles.

But this statement is strong for the refutation of new dogmas which never have existed in the church, such as those of the Manichaeans, who have thought up new absurdities. Indeed, in order for dogmas that are necessary for piety to exist, they must have existed from the very beginning in the preaching of the apostles. Therefore new dogmas and those not at all known to the apostolic church are to be rejected. But concerning Augustine's statement a rather full dispute has been made elsewhere. For a certainty, he does not concede to the church the authority of decision contrary to the Word of God, or of abolishing articles which have been handed down in the Word of God, or of establishing new articles of faith.

Enumeration of Synods

I shall bring together examples of several of the synods and of the fathers, so that it may be apparent that in them contradictory subject matter is to be found, lest without discrimination all of the sayings of all of them or all of the rites of the ancients should be accepted as necessary. Similarly there are certain foolish persons who so admire antiquity as to wish all ancient human rites restored, just as the Spartans might wish to restore all the ancient practices of their republic, although the practices instituted by men are partly defective and even if commendable, only partly congruent with other periods.

The Synod of Neo-Caesarea forbids priests to attend the feasts in celebration of second marriages lest they should seem to approve of them. Many such ridiculous regulations have been mingled with good ones. Wherefore a distinction must be made, and we must not rashly approve all the sayings of the ancients.

In the year of our Lord 324 the Synod of Nicea was convoked by Constantine. Eustathius, Bishop of Antioch, presided. In this synod very serious controversies about dogmas were settled and the errors of Paul of Samosata and of Arius were rightly condemned, as well as those of the Cathari, who denied that the fallen ought to be received again and who also denied that the fallen could attain to the remission of sins.

Subsequently certain civil arrangements were instituted about the government of the churches, so that the Bishop of Alexandria presided over the churches of the East and the Bishop of Rome over the churches of the neighboring nations. Likewise it was decided that bishops were to be ordained by neighboring bishops. These civil measures, although useful, were not meant to be considered as articles of faith.

In the third place, they added certain ceremonials, namely, the canons of penance, as they called them, which at first were not too difficult and perhaps contained very little of superstition. But subsequently the burden itself increased, superstition increased, and the idea of free pardon was obscured. Wherefore, in this respect, the fathers were not cautious enough, and since results subsequently show that superstitions increase by such examples, let us not so admire the synod in this matter that we wish either to approve or to restore such canons. Nor do we on that account disagree with the ancient church; we retain the articles of the synods about dogmas which properly pertain to the church. The others, which are either outside of or contrary to the Word of God, do not pertain to the church.

In the year of our Lord 383 there was convoked by Theodosius the Synod of Contantinople, over which the Bishop of Constantinople presided. At this time a weighty controversy was settled concerning the Holy Spirit to the effect that he is a person proceeding from the Father and the Son and is God. Eunomius and others who had been of a contrary opinion were rightly condemned. Also certain civil measures were instituted to the end that bishops were not to administer anything in the diocese of another bishop.

In the year 433 the Synod of Ephesus was convoked by Theodosius the Younger, and over it Cyril of Alexandria presided. This synod rightly condemned Nestorius, who denied that the Word was united in Christ to his human nature in a substantial union but held that the Word was only present and was dwelling in the human nature much as a guest in a domicile, in order that he might be effectual there.

This was a controversy of great importance. For in Christ the two natures are truly and substantially united; nor is it true that the human nature alone is Christ and is the domicile for the Word standing by. From this view the pious have urged these forms of speaking about the unity of the person: God was born, suffered, etc. However, although Nestorius denied that he agreed with Paul of Samosata, nevertheless I suspect that he actually felt the same way, but as a pretense he set forth the same old madness dressed up in other garments.

In the year 452 the Synod of Chalcedon was convoked by Marcian the Emperor. In this Eutyches was rightly condemned for denying even the two natures in Christ and for contending that the very nature of the Word was divinely sent and was brought forth by the Virgin and that the two natures were not a unity. It seems that here also the madness of Paul of Samosata has been renewed, but set forth in another wrapper. This decision of the synod is to be highly praised.

But by now human traditions were on the increase in the church. For that reason this synod added some corrupt regulations, not about dogmas but about ceremonies and practices beyond Scripture. Nevertheless, these regulations are still more modest than others which subsequently came into existence. In this synod the regulation was first made that prohibits the marriage of monks and virgins who have made vows, and excommunicates such persons if they contract marriages, although the mitigation is added that even this is to be left to the judgment of the bishop.

Many useful political measures were instituted at this time, such as that bishops themselves should not have the administration of ecclesiastical property, but that churches should have stewards so that no one would have too many ministries. Likewise it was decided that no one should be ordained without a ministry and that bishops in each province should assemble yearly and hold synods about the controversies existing in the church.

The adversaries keep these useful decrees of the synods secret, while they make known other less important ones, so that they seem to set the authority of the ancient church against us.

Meanwhile there have been other synods, either provincial or more frequent ones, in which the bishops of neighboring provinces convened. Of such a kind was the Synod of Antioch before the Synod of Nicea, convoked against Paul of Samosata, which piously and rightly condemned the wickedness of this man. Of such a nature likewise was the Synod of Gangra in Galatia, ancient and pure, which made the very best decrees against the superstitions about marriage, foods, and monasticism. And it appears that this synod was convened because of Montanus, Marcion, and the like, who were greatly strengthening these superstitions.

Other synods followed later, such as the one held in Anchira, which established a worthy regulation to the effect that if deacons in their ordination have not promised to live as celibates, they must be retained in their ministerial offices even though they subsequently marry. But if they have promised to become celibates and afterwards marry, they are to be removed from the ministerial office. It has other dangerous and superstitious canons also about the years of penance.

The Synod of Laodicea rightly condemns the Novatians, but it errs in censuring twice married persons, even though they be laymen. It orders them to be punished for being admitted to Communion and even prohibits Baptism after two weeks of Quadragesima. Other honorable civil measures were taken by this synod, such as the prohibition of marriages with heretics. This synod followed the Synod of Nicea by a short interval.

The first Synod of Toledo, held under Emperor Honorius, drew up many useful points of doctrine. It reviewed piously the articles about the divinity and natures of Christ and some other matters. Subsequently it touched upon some civil matters, such as the ceremonies dealing with unction and vows. This synod prohibits deacons from being elevated to the office of elder if they do not abstain from their lawful wives. Likewise it excommunicates parents who receive with parental affection their daughters who have been obligated by vows, if they later marry. Furthermore, it does not admit these married daughters to Communion unless they forsake their husbands.

The fifth Synod of Carthage held in the year 438 prohibits bishops, elders, and deacons, to have intercourse with lawful wives. Thus by degrees the prohibition was extended. Before this, intercourse with wives was conceded to deacons, as the Synod of Anchira testifies. Subsequently this, too, was prohibited. From this time on, regulations about celibacy were repeated in every synod and more severe penalties were added, such as the ones instituted by the Synod of Toledo, that the property of wives is to be sold if they return to their husbands.

Moreover, the Synod of Carthage established also another regulation worthy to be mentioned. It relates to chapels and altars for saints where their bodies have not been buried. The bishop ordered the altars and chapels to be torn down or, if there was danger of uprisings, the bishops were ordered in their addresses to dissuade people from frequenting these places. It is apparent that some persons wanted to check the growing superstition in the worship of the saints.

The Synod of Carthage, held in the year 457, had to do with
the appeals of bishops. The Roman pontiff demanded that appeal
should be granted wherever anyone appealed to the Roman pontiff.
To accomplish this he committed a fraud, citing a false decree
which he affirmed had been brought forth in respect to this judgment by the Synod of Nicea. Afterwards, from examples sought
from the Synod of Constantinople, the deception was detected and
the request of the Roman pontiff was repudiated. Augustine was
present at this synod. By such devices the Roman pontiffs constructed their way to primacy. This example warns that we should
not so admire antiquity that we free it from all vices.

The fourth Synod of Carthage contains a decree about prayer
and oblation for the dead in these words: "As for penitents who
have diligently kept the canons of penance, in case of death before
communion, let their memory be cared for by prayers and oblations." There was at this time no such thing as a private mass, but
the superstition had gradually grown. This canon does not include
the dead unless the rites of penance have been diligently observed.
Likewise it adds the custom of oblations.

The Synod of Milevita, attended by Augustine, treated a very important matter. Augustine rightly defended the doctrines of original
sin, grace, and justification. The synod also considered some civil
matters, among which these decrees are noteworthy. It forbids
appeal to transmarine bishops. This was now decreed lest a certain
Roman bishop receive an appeal. It also forbids that judges who are
not bishops be sought from the emperor. That was in agreement
with the times, but it would now be difficult. Concerning divorce
also it made a decree to the effect that the innocent party not
contract marriage again and added that the emperor was to be
petitioned to make a law in keeping with this opinion. This, too,
is rather difficult. For Fabiola at Rome contracted another marriage,
as it appears from Jerome.

This synod also confirms the superstition about vows and assents
to virgins being veiled before the twenty-fifth year, in direct opposition to older canons. Accordingly, although it made tolerable
pronouncements about doctrine, nevertheless some subsequent
regulations and superstitious rulings were agreed upon. Wherefore
not all of the decrees of synods are to be approved indiscriminately.
And still it must be granted that devout synods are well deserving,
since they preserved some articles of Christian doctrine and held
fast to the testimony of synods and of antiquity.

Ecclesiastical Writers of Antiquity

These also are well deserving, especially to the extent in which they are witnesses of the ancient and primitive church of the apostles. For they confirm our position by their testimony on the following points: the Trinity, the natures in Christ, infant Baptism, the use of the Lord's Supper, the ordination of ministers, the marriage of ministers, the use of adiaphora, the repentance of the fallen. On all of these articles, noteworthy examples from the apostles which support our position are quoted.

On the other hand, some writers in some matters and others in different ones have been rather diligent and, as is only human, they often pour forth rashly both foolish and false opinions, which, had they been admonished, they undoubtedly would have had to correct. Often, although they did not think badly, nevertheless they could not express in a sufficiently clear manner just what they wanted to say. Often because of the custom of the times they defended their timely traditions rather harshly. At times they even held some false opinions. Wherefore not all of the writings of the fathers are to be approved without discrimination; and often they fight among themselves. Nor is it a rare thing that someone even differs with himself. Consequently, the final decision ought to rest within apostolic Scripture. But I am submitting some examples.

Origen

When Origen cites examples and opinions from the apostles and the ancient churches, he is a useful witness to posterity on some of the articles: the Trinity, the two natures in Christ, infant Baptism, original sin, the use of the Lord's Supper and certain other articles. But he has mingled with his writings false and absurd opinions, some of which even his own age derided. He imagines that there have been more worlds before this world. He thinks that there will be an end to the punishments of the devils and of the damned. Such teachings as these even his own age repudiated.

When he treats the proposition in Romans that we are justified by faith and not by works, he understands the statement by synecdoche: We are justified by faith, that is, by a perfect faith embracing all of the virtues. And this he declares, saying that the same can be said of other virtues. We are justified by mercy—of course, perfect mercy which embraces other virtues. But this is no different from saying that men possess the remission of their sins for the sake of their works and their own virtues and are just. And since he does not consider what Paul is doing, what he calls faith, or why he wants the exclusive term "not by works," Origen adds confused and perplexed interpretations, and he is not consistent with himself.

Now and then he pours forth some tolerable statement, but soon afterwards he spoils it. Such, for example, is the passage on Romans 4, where he says that the beginning of justification by God is faith which believes in him who is justifying. And this faith, when it has been justified, just as a root sustained by water is fixed fast in the soil of the soul so that when it has begun to be cultivated by the Law of God, branches spring forth in it which bear the fruits of works. Therefore the root of righteousness is not from works, but the fruit of works grows out of the root—to be sure, that root of righteousness by which God makes our righteousness without works acceptable to himself.

On the third chapter of Romans, where it says: "Where is thy glory?" he now seems nearer to Paul's view and admits the exclusive aspect that men are justified by faith alone and adduces the examples of the thief on the cross and of the woman in Luke, to whom Christ says, "Thy faith hath made thee whole." But after declaring these things, it seems that he means to say that man at the beginning attains the remission of sins by faith alone. Subsequently he is made righteous by other virtues, just as he himself later says: "Faith is reckoned as righteousness to him who is converted, but afterwards righteousness is reckoned as righteousness." Then there is a strange variety and perplexity of interpretation. And although he concedes that man at the beginning attains the remission of sins by faith alone, nevertheless, if he afterwards imagines that the converted are without sin, satisfy the Law, and are made righteous for the sake of other virtues, he certainly disagrees with Paul and with the rest of the divine Scriptures, as is seen from this: "No living soul will be justified in thy sight." Likewise: "If we say that we have no sin . . ."

On Chapter 7 of Romans he clearly says that the saints represent another person when they attribute sin to themselves, as in Daniel: "Not in our own righteousness, but in thy mercy wilt thou hear us." He corrupts such statements and teaches reliance on self-righteousness of what amounts to despair. On the third chapter he says: " 'The righteousness of God has been made manifest without the law,' that is, outside of the natural law new evangelical laws have been handed down, such as this: 'Let not your right hand know what your left hand does.'" This law, he says, was before unknown. Likewise: "The law is spiritual," he understands only in an allegorical sense, that is, the ceremonies have the property of an allegory. And often he understands the Spirit unsatisfactorily; he does not understand the movements of the Holy Spirit, but only allegorical interpretation or reflection.

On Romans 8 where it reads: "That which was impossible for the law because it was made weak through the flesh," he transfers flesh to the word law, that is, the flesh of the law was weak, meaning, of course, that the ceremonies were impossible, useless, etc. But Paul understands by flesh the very nature of man. The Law was rendered weak by the flesh, that is, the Law could not be kept by human nature. These references show that Origen runs off course and does not pay attention to what Paul is doing.

I could collect many lesser passages, as for instance, when Origen says that Peter excels the others because a plural was used in addressing him: ". . . it will be loosed in the *heavens*." The singular is used in addressing the whole company of the apostles: ". . . shall be loosed in *heaven*." But I omit such futile things. Otherwise it is good for those who are learned and who employ reason to read the writings of the ancients, first of all, for the sake of their historical testimonies and then because a comparison sharpens the wits of the studious and gives them good exercise. A reading of Origen will be good for those who have been rightly instructed beforehand and who hold the sum of Christian doctrine.

Dionysius

There is one small book by Dionysius, *Ecclesiastical Hierarchy*, which is useful for its history. Other works contain casual speculations. But in the work just cited ceremonies of the Sacraments and rites of the church are handed down, and it appears that ceremonies at that time were still moderate. But especially the rites of the mass are to be considered in that work, so it appears that the more recent rites in the pope's church have departed far from the ancient form. Certain Psalms and Gospel lectionaries used to be recited, and prayers were said for the church and the state. After this, the elder stood at the altar and recited the words of Christ in the Lord's Supper. Then he distributed the Sacrament to the people. Then followed the prayer of thanksgiving. This was the rite of the mass, and it is clear from this that the mass was only a Communion and that there were no private masses. But that is the thing to be marvelled at, that no mention is made of an offering, nor does he relate any rite whatsoever of one offering up anything. It is especially good to observe these things in Dionysius, in order that we may place antiquity over against those who defend the abuse of masses.

He tells about Baptism, anointing, Communion, as I have said, and the ordination of elders and of those who were making vows. He mentions also the anointing of the dead, telling what the ceremonies were at funerals when the corpse had been placed in the sanctuary and certain selections from sacred Scripture about the resurrection were read in the presence of the people. Then the people were adjoined to give thanks in prayers because the deceased had piously departed with a knowledge of the Gospel. There was added an exhortation that each person should pray for a devout departure from this life. This custom was full of piety and worthy of praise. For what greater blessings can be conceived than to retain a knowledge of Christ in the great agony of death and to be assisted and saved by Christ? This better ceremony has been completely destroyed by a more recent age and worse ones have indeed been retained and piled up.

Dionysius adds that after this exhortation the elder turned aside and sprinkled the corpse with oil, praying that God would forgive any weakness which had remained in him after his conversion. Subsequently the corpse was placed in the ground. These were the only funeral ceremonies at that time, and still no mention was made of the dead in the mass. Much less was the body of the Lord offered up for the dead. This defilement of the Sacrament has been added by a later age.

Thus far I have spoken of Dionysius, in whom, although ceremonies are somewhat less corrupt, we see nevertheless the beginnings of monasticism. And this fact is worthy of serious reproof, that he does not discern between the Sacraments, which have been divinely instituted, and the traditions of men. He speaks of anointing quite as he speaks of Baptism and equates non-essentials with essentials, so to speak. He even prefers the ordination of monks to that of ministers, which is a matter strongly to be condemned, since the ordination of ministers pertains to the preaching of the Gospel, but the ordination of monks is full of superstition and is done only because of a practice prohibited according to the passage which reads: "In vain do they worship me with the mandates of men." And yet in Dionysius monasticism is called perfection. There-

fore, let his testimonies prevail because they relate to history, in
order that we may know what rites were in use at that time, not that
dogmas or laws may be established according to his descriptions.

Tertullian

Tertullian rightly refuted Marcion and the rest of the heretics
of that party. Tertullian's works contain useful testimonies on the
Trinity, and he relates, not his own opinion, but the ancient one
accepted by the apostles. Against Praxeas there is extant his shining
witness to the Word, that is, the Son of God, to the effect that he
is a person even before he assumed human nature.

But even the ancients reprove some of his errors, namely, his
condemnation of second marriages and his ridiculous argument to
this effect: It is not permitted to marry the wife of a dead brother.
He who marries a widow left by a Christian is actually marrying
the wife of a dead brother. Therefore he does wrong in so doing.
He makes sport of the reign of saints also, which they imagined
would endure a thousand years in this bodily life before the world
conflagration and before the last judgment, with some in turn
rising from the grave rather quickly, others, quite slowly. This
Jewish nonsense ought to be blasted out of the church.

In a little book, *The Crown of a Soldier,* he says many things
about human rites and blusters most harshly about sexual relations
and the fact that they must be according to law. Since these sayings in the church have been grossly distorted, as it happens, great
errors in all ages would be affirmed, since human beings never
have such vigilance that some vicious relations do not take them by
surprise.

However, Tertullian relates some rather puerile customs, for
example that one should not take a bath for seven days after Baptism. Likewise, to those baptized it was customary to offer milk and
honey as a snack. He also says: "We make each year offerings for
the dead as birthday presents." Now these are irreverently distorted by our adversaries into masses for the dead. Why do they
omit birthdays if they attribute so much to the authority of Tertullian? But he does not speak about the Lord's Supper. But on
birthdays and at funerals food and other gifts were customarily
carried into the temples for the poor. These they called offerings
and love feasts, and the custom was taken over from the Gentiles,
but somewhat reformed. For the Gentiles used to give sumptuous

banquets, even in the temples, on birthdays and at funeral occasions, but later on the Synod of Nicea and other synods forbade such ostentation on birthdays.

Therefore, as has been said about others, the historical testimonies of Tertullian are valuable when he speaks of what the earlier church thought. But let not his expositions and arguments be received as though they were dogmas, except in so far as they are in agreement with apostolic Scripture.

Cyprian

Cyprian lived about the year of our Lord 260. He has useful testimonies on the following: the Trinity, infant Baptism, the use of the Lord's Supper, and the form of the election of bishops. The bishops were elected by the assembly of the church, he writes, and the election was approved by several neighboring bishops who had been assembled.

But the ancients also censured Cyprian because he felt that persons who had been baptized by heretics must be baptized a second time. He pours forth, in the midst of his blustering, occasional foolish judgments, when he exaggerates with excessive hyperbole the cause which he espouses. For example, he writes quite harshly about canonic penalties and says that absolution has no value unless the penalties have been completely met. How much wrong this statement contains is not hard to see. He also clamors strongly about celibacy, although, to be sure, he softens this passage by ordering those very persons who had made vows, to contract marriage if they should not keep their promise. In a little book, *On Alms*, he says that sins committed before Baptism are remitted for the sake of the Passion of Christ, but after Baptism remission must be sought through the giving of alms. These statements are full of nonsense. Although admonished about them, he would by no means have corrected them. Therefore not all of his statements are to be considered as dogmas.

Concerning the Lord's Supper he customarily uses the words "offering" and "sacrifice," just as others who speak carelessly: We offer up prayers, we offer up bread, wine, we offer up the body and blood of Christ. Such terminology we meet also in Cyprian. From this source our enemies assume proofs for the profanation of the Lord's Supper in private mass, etc.

Great is the power of custom, and in following it men often

speak improperly, even as we now say "mass" when no one knows
the etymology of the term. In such a manner the ancients held fast
to the words "offering" and "sacrifice," without too much care as
to the etymology and proper meaning of the words. But because
Augustine saw something unsuitable in these terms, he himself
softens them by saying that it is to be called sacrifice "as a reminder
of the sacrifice," and offering "as a reminder of the offering." These
are metonymies, just as we say that the Paschal Lamb is a reminder
or sign of the passing over. But I am unwilling either cleverly to
interpret or to apologize for the customary manner of speech of
that time. For thus the people spoke who now and then received
an improper word.

Irenaeus clearly states that this offering is a giving of thanks.
Others judged likewise, as the word "Eucharist" bears out. Wherefore, they have felt it to be a ceremony in which thanks are expressed. There is nothing unsuitable in this. For we accept the view
that we should be reminded of the blessing given to us by Christ
and we should kindle our faith, and then give thanks for this
blessing. But it does not follow from this that this is a work to be
done for others or to be applied to the good of others, etc. Such
monstrous ideas as these were not even thought of by the fathers.
Therefore, when we read the words "sacrifice" and "offering," let
us understand by them either a sign of the sacrifice and offering
or the giving of thanks, and not imagine them to be applications in
behalf of others.

Sometimes the whole operation that takes place at the altar is
called by the one name "offering," namely both prayers and the
Supper of the Lord. When this is done, let prayers be understood
to be the offerings.

Again, in Cyprian certain words are read about the dead which
more recent authors badly distort: "We offer sacrifices for them";
but these things he says concerning the martyrs. For mention was
being made of them in prayers when thanks were returned unto
God because he had assisted them. As the Greek canon says: "We
offer for the patriarchs, prophets, the apostles, that is, we give
thanks for them because from the beginning thou hast chosen for
thyself, redeemed, and sanctified the church from their number."
In the beginning this was the meaning of these words, and it was
not being petitioned that God should relax the punishments of the
dead. In a subsequent time evil opinions were added and in part
former words were changed, while in part the form of ancient

words was retained, so that posterity understood something different from that which the ancients had understood by these words.

Therefore the testimonies of antiquity do not support the more recent abuses. Some of these testimonies are foreign to our present customs, and others, if they have any faulty elements, ought not to be put up against the sure testimonies of Scripture, because the remaining ages also have had their own faults. This is my response to the words "offering" and "sacrifice," in a most simple manner and without sophistry.

Basil

In Basil are extant useful testimonies about the Trinity and repentance, made when he argues against Novatus. In a sermon on humility he propounds an illustrious opinion about the righteousness of faith, which clearly supports our view. Without any sophistry, he takes away justification from good works, speaking not of ceremonials but of all the virtues. He not only speaks of virtues before renewal, but also of virtues in those who have been renewed, and orders us to perceive that we are justified by reliance alone upon the mercy promised for Christ's sake.

These are his very words: "The apostle says: 'He that glorieth, let him glory in the Lord,' saying that 'to us Christ has been made by God our wisdom, and righteousness, sanctification, and redemption, and as it is written, He who will glory, let him glory in the Lord.' For this is perfect and true glorying in God when no one is puffed up on account of his own righteousness and knows that he lacks true righteousness in himself but is justified by faith alone in Christ. Paul glories in the fact that he despises his own righteousness, but seeks by faith through Christ that righteousness which is from God."

These words are sufficient to show that Basil understood the righteousness of faith in such a way that we must realize that we are righteous, that is, accepted, by faith for the sake of Christ through the mercy of God, and not for the sake of our own virtues.

Basil was the first to organize companies of monks. This example was harmful and did some injury, even though he himself at first did not have crass superstitions, and these groups still had some likeness to schools. There are even in circulation some books bearing his name, giving rules for the monks. Some of these books are without doubt not genuine but came into existence a long time after Basil. They are full of false opinions about celibacy and about

other observances thought up without the command of God. They
contain ridiculous trifles, such as a large pile of penalties or satisfactions, which he calls penalties *(epitimia)*. For instance, he says:
"If a girl in the choir laughs, let her sit for two days in the entrance
to the church." Similar dirges he sings, which, if anyone out of admiration for antiquity wanted them renewed, he would indeed be
out of his mind.

Gregory Nazianzen

Nazianzen discussed the article on the Trinity and lightly touched
upon other dogmas. He wrote the *Life of Cyprian*, in which he
relates that a certain young lady whom Cyprian loved before his
conversion invoked the Virgin Mary and thereby conquered the
magical enchantments of Cyprian.

This example is quoted as an argument for praying to the saints.
Although it seems to be a false story subsequently circulated under
the title of Nazianzen, nevertheless, even if the story were true, it
must not be cited for establishing the invocation of the saints. For
the errors of the pious must not be placed over against the Word
of God, since in every age even the devout in the church have their
characteristic weaknesses.

They assert also, on the authority of Basil and Nazianzen, that
at the end of sermons on the saints it is their custom to address
them as follows: "O Athanasius, pray for us." Although these
apostrophes can be rationalized as rhetorical figures, nevertheless
it is possible that they then invoked the saints according to the
custom of their age. For the invocation of saints was creeping into
the church by degrees at that time. Indeed, errors of the times drag
men away, just as the force of a river carries with it those who are
sailing. Consequently people disapprove the customary less than
they excuse it. But this is not a reason for approving the invocation of the saints. Since this custom has grown and its wickedness
has already been detected, it ought to be entirely rooted from the
church. Basil says nothing about invocation of the saints but only
states that the memory of saints is to be celebrated so that we may
imitate their virtues. He calls the saints helpers of our prayers, not
in the sense that they are to be invoked, but because all of the
blessed in heaven pray for the church and commend it unto God.

Epiphanius writes that certain women, as they invoked the Virgin
Mary, used to walk around her statue. He condemns this whole

procedure and calls it a work of idolatry. Epiphanius' works contain refutations of ancient heresies, especially heresies about the Trinity and a few other matters. I think that he ought to be read, especially as a historian, to be sure.

Chrysostom

The age of Chrysostom had adopted many already vicious customs which he, in taking note of them, does not censure. For example, he praises those making journeys to the monuments of the saints, and he makes mention also of prayers for the dead. He adorns monasticism with excessive and false praises. In a treatise on repentance, in which he assembles many methods of attaining the remission of sins—namely, alms, tears, and other works—he nevertheless does not mention faith, concerning which he ought to have spoken. That writing contains many false notions and is confused and full of perplexities.

The Greeks have praised highly his commentaries on Paul, in which, in the passages on justification and on faith, the logic of the Pauline argument constrains him to repeat often this judgment, that by faith we attain unto the remission of sins for Christ's sake, not for our works' sake. And he says clearly that not only is God loved by faith, but in turn believers feel that they are loved by God although they are guilty in many ways.

In this statement he has given sufficient evidence that he understands that faith is not only a matter of a knowledge of history but of that reliance by which we believe our sins are forgiven. And indeed he distinguishes this faith from works, from not stealing, from not killing, etc., and he says that this manner of life is more excellent. But although his explanation is simpler and purer than Origen's, nevertheless it is obscure and it is not entirely consistent.

In Chapter 7 he strays rather far afield when he says that concupiscence and passion, unless they produce an external act, are not sins. Nevertheless, anyone that reads his commentaries with attention and thought will discover testimonies to many articles. Although at that time there was much obscurity in the church, it still appears that there were many who retained this common view, that the remission of sins is granted by faith for the sake of Christ and not because of works. Therefore, although the ancients at times speak in a manner that is not too explicit, nevertheless in other places we can understand precisely what they intended to say.

Concerning the Lord's Supper Chrysostom makes it clear enough that there were no private masses, for he describes the elder standing at the altar and calling the people to approach the Communion.

In a little book, *On the Dignity of the Priesthood,* he distinguishes in a learned way between civil and ecclesiastical power and denies that ecclesiastical authority has the right to coerce by corporal force.

Ambrose

Ambrose touches on many subjects, such as the Trinity in his refutation of the Novatians, and on justification. In his commentaries, which seem to be not so much written by him as to be excerpts from others, some contradictory statements are found. Nevertheless it is clear from his longer discussions that he taught about grace and justification exactly what we teach. A witness to this fact is his *Epistle to Irenaeus,* in which he treats Paul's statement that "the law works wrath . . ." (Epistle 71), speaking thus: " 'By the works of the Law no man is justified,' that is, through the Law sin is known, but guilt is not mitigated. Therefore the Lord Jesus by his coming has forgiven all men the sin which no one could avoid, and, by the shedding of his blood, has blotted out the handwriting against us. That is to say, 'Sin superabounded through the law, but grace superabounded through Jesus Christ,' just as John says: 'Behold the Lamb of God that taketh away the sins, etc.' Therefore, let no man glory in works because no man is justified by his works. Whoever is justified possesses justification as a gift since he is justified by Christ. Faith, therefore, is that which liberates us through Christ's blood, for that person is blessed whose sin is forgiven and to whom pardon is granted."

But some similar views are discovered in other passages of this writer, as in his *Calling of the Gentiles.* Furthermore, in his *Epistle to Demetrias the Virgin* he states: "For no other reason is a rule given except to secure aid from the one who gives it." But under his name are extant certain selections on preparation for the mass and some other meaningless writings which are apparent forgeries.

Jerome

In his translations Jerome has performed a great work for the church and, although his interpretations of the prophets are rather poor, nevertheless his exposition of the histories, which is taken from the ancients, is useful. He wrote very little about dogmas. In writing against Jovinian he strongly confirms false and superstitious opinions about human traditions. He disparages marriage and rails at it with abusive language, which is by no means worthy of a Christian. He collects badly distorted passages of Scripture as if they disparage marriage, such as: "If you live according to the flesh, you shall die," and similar passages. He expressly states that there is no difference between one who marries a second time and a prostitute. Likewise, he says that we must observe not what God allows but what he wills, as though God does not will marriage. Finally, in a Gentile manner he gathers together the vulgar criticisms of the female sex and married life, concerning which a Christian, who knows that the reason for the weakness of both sexes is corrupt human nature, ought to feel entirely otherwise. The Christian knows that, in spite of man's nature, honor ought to be attributed to the woman for God's sake. Since God has not in vain ordained this sex, it ought to be recognized as a work of God and the divine order must be greatly honored. There is no less weakness of soul in the male in matters that are committed to him. Moreover, because of love for God a Christian bears and alleviates weakness in his associates in this life who have been divinely joined to him and are joint-heirs of glory. He knows that God wills that we should care for women as a part of the human race, nor should we despise them with diabolical haughtiness. These and other statements about this matter ought rather to have been spoken in a Christian argument than those scurrilous censures of the sex and the divine order.

On the subject of the choice of foods he praises rites which have been instituted without reference to the Word of God, as though they were a worship of God, rather, as though they were perfection itself. It is a ridiculous precept he puts down when he says: "If you want to be perfect, it is good not to drink wine and not to eat flesh." Here he wretchedly distorts a statement of Paul, who says, "It is good not to eat meat," but adds, "if it offends thy brother." Now, although such superstitions in the church must be censured, for they produce many other errors, one must deliberate prudently about such inconsiderate statements.

In a dialogue against Pelagius he rightly argues that renewal is not brought about only by the powers of free will, but that there is need for the help of the Holy Spirit. He also correctly denies that the saints are without sin and puts down a noteworthy statement

as follows: "We are justified at the moment we confess that we
are sinners, and our righteousness is not by our own merit but
comes by the mercy of God." But later on he does not say clearly
enough that the sins of the saints are to be understood as actual
sins, such as the fires of lust or anger, and the like. Nor does he
understand anything about inner and perpetual doubt, false security,
and concupiscence. Therefore it is clear that there are many errors
in Jerome's writings, and those errors are not small.

Augustine

Augustine dealt with many necessary controversies and in so
doing refuted the Arians, the Manichaeans, the Donatists, and the
Pelagians. For there had crept into the church already many philosophical opinions which Pelagius strengthened, transforming the
Gospel into a philosophy. Pelagius contended that there was no
original sin, that men could satisfy the law of God, and that they
merited remission of sins by their external obedience, that men were
righteous and merited eternal life. He said nothing about faith in
Christ, nothing about the aid of the Holy Spirit. This doctrine
of Pelagius was not evangelical but philosophical. In like manner
the judgment of the scholastic doctors means the same thing, except
that these doctors sew on something of monastic superstitions. And
now again many are slipping back into the views of Pelagius because they seem plausible to their reason.

Augustine in his age restored the doctrine of the Gospel of grace
and rekindled a faith that was almost extinct. For this service the
church is greatly indebted to him. He speaks with much more
clarity about original sin than all the rest. He talks more clearly
and correctly, too, about free will. For he says that men by the
powers of free will can do the external works of the Law and
honorable civil works but without the Holy Spirit they cannot have
spiritual impulses such as true fear of God, true trust, true patience,
that is, that newness which ought to exist in those who are to
be saved.

He transmits a useful distinction between the letter and the Spirit
and teaches free remission of sins, warning us just as Paul must be
understood to have done, when he says: "By the works of the law
no man is justified." For example, he not only separates justification
from ceremonials, but also from moral works. There was a great
need of such an admonition in the church. For Origen and many

who followed him had disseminated a false interpretation in the church in that they separated justification from ceremonies only; they imagined that men satisfied the Law and were justified because of works. Therefore Augustine treats this question in a learned fashion in a book on *The Spirit and the Letter* and affirms the fact that Paul everywhere includes the moral law when he denies that men are justified by the Law. Likewise he denies that men satisfy the Law (Romans 8).

This admonition of Augustine, and this passage of his, highly deserve to be remembered, for since reason does not see clearly the magnitude of original sin and of corrupt human nature, it easily falls into such opinions so that it thinks it can satisfy the Law and that men are righteous because of works. Thus the righteousness of faith is obscured and lost from the scene, and true spiritual exercises are discarded, namely, true prayer, which ought to rely on mercy alone. Even so we are now derided by our opponents, who want to seem wiser, and they loudly proclaim that we are foolishly exaggerating human weakness and that we in a ridiculous manner are distinguishing between justification and works, while reason understands that righteousness is nothing else than obedience according to the Law.

But the Gospel doctrine about sin and the righteousness of faith is a hidden and peculiar wisdom of the true church, which even a few of the writers have recognized; and it is the saner ones who have done so, some in a rather obscure manner; others, in a rather clear manner. The Scotists and the like have entirely covered it over. Therefore, after God has revealed it again, let us guard diligently this illustrious doctrine.

Furthermore, why do not our adversaries, on the other hand, consider how absurd it is to say that Christ has freed us only from the ceremonial laws. Likewise, if the liberation pertains only to the ceremonial laws, then it was of no value to the fathers before Moses' time. But it is necessary to conclude that the emancipation from the law pertains to the whole church from the very beginning even to the end of the world. These topics are most fully discussed, as I have said, in the book by Augustine, *The Spirit and the Letter*.

Finally, those who think that emancipation from the law pertains only to ceremonial laws are entirely ignorant of what emancipation from the law means. Just as all men after Adam's fall were oppressed with sin, with the wrath of God, with tremendous hardships of life, and with eternal punishments, just so are all burdened down with the Law, which reveals sin, condemns us, and slays us with everlasting terrors. It is as Paul says: Therefore, to be freed from the Law is to be freed from that verdict that we are subject to the wrath of God and eternal death. It is to be liberated, not only from rites or external spectacles, but much more to be delivered from the Law which completely terrifies, curses, damns, and slays us, when, to be sure, another factor is proposed because of which we are pronounced righteous, namely the Son of God who has been made a victim for us.

In such a manner Adam, Noah, Abraham, and all the elect before Moses were liberated from the Law. They were condemned by the Law and were afflicted with horrible terrors and with a sense of the wrath and the curse of God. But in the midst of these terrors they were raised up by the acceptance of mercy promised for the sake of the coming Lord and they concluded that they were pronounced righteous because of a coming victim, not because of the Law. They had recognized that sins are not only outer transgressions but also inner uncleanness, horrible doubt about God, murmuring and indignation against God in adversity, as well as other depraved impulses. And they knew that their sin itself and the weakness of nature were not removed by some law, nor was the wrath of God, but they knew that they were saved from such terrors by the acceptance of and the reliance on a Savior who had been promised.

So these men were freed from the Law, it is clear, as it judged and slew them, and from the eternal wrath of God which the Law announces. They knew from natural knowledge that free remission of sins was not declared. Therefore they sought remission from some other source. If they had felt that they would be righteous only when they were without fault, they would have succumbed in agony of conscience. But they knew that a Savior had been promised for the very reason that they might conclude that they pleased God even if they were unworthy and unclean. Thus they felt themselves to be righteous, not because of the Law but because of a coming Savior.

Freedom from the Law embraces such great things as these, which are not understood by undisturbed individuals who do not know what true repentance or prayer is and who are not belabored by afflictions, and who either have souls occupied with pleasures or are taking delight in their opinions, while spurning the Word of God, or inflating and corrupting their own imaginations.

Some of our shrewder opponents, although they see that Augustine's and our interpretation is the opinion of Paul and of prophetic and apostolic Scripture, nevertheless cry out against us and cite the authority of Origen, Jerome, Chrysostom, and I know not whom else. It is not that they truly and heartily approve of them, but only that they might deceive the inexperienced so that they might not appear to be defeated. For our opponents do not bring to these contests a good conscience and an interest in the quest for truth, but a hatred of us, contempt for the Gospel, and an anxiety for maintaining their own authority. What the people feel about Christ, how the churches are to be instructed, they judge in no way pertains to them. In part they openly employ a sycophant like Cochlaeus or Witzel and men like them, who are partly satellites of tyranny and of the tyrants, who, because of a reputation for wisdom or for virtue, direct the counsels of pontiffs, kings, and princes, although they are godless men who generally think that religions are false. And they themselves are pleased in such an extraordinary manner by that name that they would even dare to resist thunder, as the comic poet Aristophanes says. And they would express such opinions at the synods about the glory of Christ, whose name they think is fabulous.

Accordingly, I urge pious readers first to consider the kinds of doctrine and then simply and without sophistry to declare the opinion of prophetic and apostolic Scripture. Then when the fathers are cited, they should see that they use statements which are in agreement with the divine voice. For there is great disagreement among the fathers. Finally, as Paul orders us to test the spirits, the intent and the substance of the counsel of each party must be observed. This our opponents do, not to improve anything, but only by some sort of pretext to defend their tyranny and to strengthen and secure their wealth. Therefore both kings and pontiffs are opposed to the marriage of priests, because they see that celibacy is more helpful for the retention of their power and wealth. In this manner, since the evidences of a wicked will are extant in some evident articles, it is clear enough that they are not motivated by the good Spirit. But they are the enemies of Christ, and in none of the rest of the articles do they seek the truth. Wherefore, let us firmly reject their opinions.

Writing on Psalm 42 Augustine declares that a person who has been born again is not righteous because of works, but by faith. He says: "If you say that you are righteous, clearly be afraid if you do not possess that word from another Psalm which reads: 'Enter not into judgment with thy servant'; for if thou wilt show thy judgment without mercy, whither shall I go? If thou shouldst mark iniquities, O Lord, who will sustain me? Enter not into judgment with thy servant, for no living soul will be justified in thy sight.' Therefore, if no living soul will be justified in thy sight—because whoever lives here, however justly he lives, woe to him if God has entered into judgment with him. For also in another one of the prophets God rebukes the arrogant and the proud in this manner: 'Why do you contend with me in judgment? All ye have forsaken me, saith the Lord; therefore, do not contend with me in judgment, but take care to be righteous.' However great you have been, confess yourself to be a sinner and hope always for mercy. In such a humble confession as this, speak more quietly to thy soul that is disturbing thee and raging against thee, 'Wherefore art thou sad, O my soul, and why dost thou disturb me?' Perhaps you wanted to hope in thyself? 'Hope thou in the Lord,' not in thyself, for what art thou in thyself and what art thou of thyself? Let that one be soundness in thee who accepts wounds for thee and says: 'Hope in the Lord.' "

On Psalm 31 he says: Who are the blessed? It is not they in whom he will find no sin, for he finds it in all. For all have sinned and lack the glory of God. If, therefore, sins are found in all, it remains that there are none blessed except those whose sins have been forgiven. This, therefore, the apostle has commended thus: "Abraham believed God and it was imputed unto him for righteousness." He rightly accommodates the statement to faith, and witnesses that he understands by faith not only a historical knowledge, but a trust by which we firmly believe that our sins are forgiven for Christ's sake. Nor, indeed, can anyone who does not thus understand the word "faith" follow the reasoning of Paul. As the saying goes, this truly is to go astray at the very door, to understand faith to be only knowledge of history, rather than trust in the mercy promised for Christ's sake. Nor is it any wonder that the monks go astray their whole lifetime in an interpretation of Paul, for on this very topic they shamefully wander. Right now this darkness is to our adversaries a special impediment to their accepting the doctrine of faith, because they do not rightly understand the word "faith."

Why do they not weigh such statements by Augustine, the like of which I have just related? Augustine bears witness that Paul means that Abraham is pronounced righteous because he believed not only about his posterity but also in the remission of sins. Such judgments, everywhere evident in Augustine, show clearly that he believes about grace and faith exactly what we teach. Just as he remarks in *The Spirit and the Letter:* "According to the Law we fear God, but through faith we flee to mercy." He discerns both Law and Gospel in a learned manner.

Now although at times in his writings there occur figures of speech which are not explicit enough or applicable, these must be condoned in view of the times, since common usage had accepted certain figures, such as the term "merit" and others which the learned could not eradicate. Then, too, the authors themselves were not accustomed enough to the use of accurate arguments, and the degree of obscurity in the church at that time can be estimated from the fact that the wicked opinion of Pelagius was accepted with such great applause that Augustine and a few others have been unable to extirpate it again from the churches without great efforts.

But concerning the question of ceremonies, if anyone brings up the age of Augustine against us, let him know that not even Augustine himself was pleased with all of the rites and opinions of his own age. For he complains that many superstitious opinions are holding fast in the church and that the traditions of man are preferred to the precepts of God. Ceremonies were piled up to such a degree that the bondage of the Jews was more tolerable than that of the church.

These were his words in the *Epistle to Januarius* (119). Nevertheless, he wanted religion itself, with as few and as clear sacramental celebrations as possible, to be free by the mercy of God. But some teachers oppress it with servile burdens, so that the law of the Jews who were subject to divine, not human, laws, was more tolerable. In the first place, Augustine says about human rites that this entire kind of thing contains free observances. Then he clearly orders useless human rites to be cut off entirely. Therefore Augustine does not so much approve of the ceremonies of his age as he wishes the church to be declared to be the norm for this purpose. For many things had been accepted which not even he himself approves; rather he wishes them censured and corrected. Certain things he observes in accordance with the practice of his day, just as all of us condone many features of present practices.

During Augustine's age sermons on purgatory were becoming very prevalent. He neither refutes nor confirms them; he only talks about them. He says that there are some who believe that the souls of pious persons are purged after they have left the bodies. But in his *Confessions* (9), he requests a prayer for his dead mother in these words: "Inspire, O Lord, thy servants to remember at the altar my mother and father." Beyond this he makes no request. Although he says this in a reverent manner, nevertheless it is now shamefully distorted into an offering of the sacrament for the dead, such as did not yet exist in Augustine's day.

But the customary vows were in existence at that time, and the question occurs whether marriages contracted after a vow had been made should be dissolved. On this question the opinion of Augustine is extant in his *Decree for Marriages* (27, Q. 1. c.).

Although in this work Augustine attributes more importance to vows than he should, nevertheless he pronounces that marriages contracted after vows ought not to be dissolved. And he affirms that they are truly marriages, since one person ought not with injury to another person return to a vow. Nor is an obligation between two persons made of none effect if one of them announces a change in a previous resolution. This in summary he says in that text. But the error in regard to vows was stronger than this mitigation of Augustine. On that account the regulations coming later broke up marriages. Augustine saw that this separation was vicious, but he did not properly consider what vice there was even in the vows themselves, which was a rather obscure thing to discern. For he was overcome by the popular opinions of his age. Already the custom of making vows had been accepted. Great was the admiration for many who lived this kind of life. However, admiration was an obstruction to good judgment. Therefore he did not dispute whether there was any value in vows. And although, to be sure, there were many errors implicit in them, they were considered to be venerations, an outstanding merit of righteousness, perfection, and likewise they were impossibilities for many people. If he had first refuted vows, he would have been better able to prohibit the separation of marriages.

It is agreed, therefore, that many abuses had, already at that time, become fixed in the church. Although Augustine was opposed to many of them, still he considered some of them good, but after they have been disclosed, they should not be defended. Then, too, even if the examples of the ancients were disguised in his age, still they should not by any means now be adapted to the confirmation of greater abuses.

Thus the conclusion is by no means valid that since Augustine orders prayer for his mother to be said at the altar, masses for the dead ought to be approved. Nor should it be said that because in Augustine's time some were of the opinion that there was a purgatory, therefore masses must be approved, as well as indulgences and other ceremonies devised for the dead. For in the time of Augustine such strange irreverences were not yet in existence, although by degrees their seeds were scattered.

Gregory

In the year 590 Gregory entered the office of the pontiff, exactly 157 years after the death of Augustine. In the meantime there had flowed into Italy many barbarian nations, the Goths, the Lombards, and their allies. Not only had there been a great decline in the pursuits of learning and great neglect of the churches, but the barbarous nations themselves, who were in possession of Italy, brought along with them or easily accepted many false opinions. Therefore, in a short time abuses greatly accumulated.

In this tearing to pieces of Italy there seemed to be a peculiar kind of happiness obtained from being away from the state, from living far away in some sort of solitude, without family, without children, and in not witnessing the destruction of cities and the devastation of the fatherland. For it is wretched to say what Aeneas said: "And of these things I was a great part." Therefore gentle people who had families were congratulating the monks upon their tranquillity. Thus admiration for monks increased, and more people began to seek and to love withdrawal from the world.

Men, barbarous by nature, began to admire these new rites which had the appearance of exceptional piety and, as it were, led to fellowship with God. It is no wonder, then, that during that time the groups of monks increased and plausible opinions about that kind of works were spread abroad more widely, while all the time the light of the Gospel of true faith and true worship became extinct.

For to the barbarians the veneration of the saints was pleasing. After it had once been accepted that in accordance with their national custom they should adorn the saints with statues and special temples, the custom increased through the imitation of those in power. By degrees this led to so much irreverence that the worship of the saints in these latter ages in no way differed from the open idolatry of the Gentiles. Anna and George were being invoked just as were Juno, Mars, or Hercules. People ran to statues, and with great authority the bishops confirmed the mania for idols while the doctors praised it. And the sum of religion came to be in such venerations as these.

Meanwhile there was great silence about the invocation of Christ and about faith. Obviously, the beginnings of such great wickedness ought to have been guarded against. But Gregory actually vigorously strengthened this evil development by instituting the public rite of the invocation of saints and by ordering temples to be dedicated to their bones and dust. Furthermore, at this time there crept into the church the practice of offering the body and blood of Christ for the dead. This practice gave birth to a horrible defilement of the Sacrament.

Although, therefore, after the age of Gregory there followed an even greater darkness, nevertheless the following errors were fixed at that time in the church: a false teaching about monasticism, about works conceived without the mandate of God, the invocation of the saints, and the offering of the body of Christ for the dead. These errors subsequently produced great disaster.

Thus the age of Gregory established no norm for correcting the church. And in order that this can be seen more readily, I shall first relate some of the more obvious errors of Gregory, and then I shall refute a few of his errors about the Lord's Supper.

In the third book of his Epistles, his *Epistle to Catanenses the Bishop of Sicily,* Gregory directs: Let not subdeacons and deacons have sexual relations with their wives whom they married before their ordination. But to be sure, before this the Sicilians had preserved the Greek custom, nor had they forbidden married persons sex relations with their mates. This error is quite evident. For no godly man can approve such separation in a legitimate marriage. He relates that there was a certain attractive fellow who preferred to quit the office of subdeacon rather than deprive himself of sex relations with his wife. This fellow, whoever he was, was endowed with saner judgment than the persons who were disrupting such unions.

The sin of Gregory becomes greater because he expected this custom to be accepted in the churches of Sicily, which to this time, according to the decrees of the ancient synods, had retained marriages in every ecclesiastical position and did not burden the deacons and others with vows. Why does Gregory take upon himself the rule

over other churches when indeed he declaims that he abhors the title
of Universal Bishop? Moreover, why does he break up marriages
where the deacons had not been burdened with vows? Why does
he not respect the authority of former synods? Since this error
contains evident wickedness and tyranny, it is clear indeed that
Gregory's age was not without its great errors.

How unjust he is, too, toward those who, by order of their parents, had been trained as children in the monasteries, and after
having become older were seeking another kind of life. About these
he remarks: It is a crime for them to quit the monastic life. Such
austerity is to be censured not only because it has done injury to
the age, but also because it has vigorously strengthened the superstitious opinions about monastic practices.

I shall add a third error that is by no means obscure. He is influenced by apparitions to approve of the offering of the Sacrament for the dead. He tells about two fellows who after death were
serving in the baths; one of them begged that an offering of the
Sacrament be made for him in order that he might be liberated
from his punishments. From these ghosts he receives dogmas in the
church contrary to the clear order of God in Deuteronomy 18: "Seek
thou not the truth from the dead." Isaiah 8 says: "Should a people
seek truth from God for the living or from the dead?" Therefore,
whatever the condition of souls is after this life, dogmas nevertheless are not to be received from ghosts. Moreover, who does not
see that he is a poet, when he says that after death the pious became bath-keepers? The story is similar to the fiction about the
daughters of Danaus, who drew water with sieves.

I have not constructed this list to increase the refutations of
their errors, many of which are extant in sufficient number elsewhere, but I have wished only to enumerate these errors to show
that they are mistaken who admire the fathers as though they have
never erred and as if they nowhere disagree with divine Scriptures.
Therefore, although the more enlightened fathers do at times admonish us in some matter, yet we must judge them in accordance
with the Word of God.

Therefore, omitting further refutations, I shall add briefly some
words about the offering for the dead. There is no need to inquire
whether there is a purgatory, for the question in no way pertains to
offering. Even if there were a purgatory, it is plain wickedness to
offer the Sacrament for the dead. And there are many very strong
reasons for this. The first is that it is a wickedness to institute an

observance in the church without God's order. This use of the Lord's Supper for the benefit of others is done without any divine order or evidence. Therefore, without any doubt, this practice is wicked.

This major premise is confirmed by very many passages. "Thou shalt have no other gods." In this mandate of the Law, "other" practices in worship are also prohibited. And to this point the statement applies: "In vain do they worship me with the mandates of men." This statement is also relevant: "Whatsoever is not of faith is sin." Moreover, observances not commanded by God cannot come into being according to faith. But the world does not understand how great a sin it is to contrive practices without an order from God and to depart from the Word of God. The prophets strongly proclaim with respect to this crime and deplore the blindness of men who with dreadful audacity fashion practices and dogmas about the will of God but do not hold fast to the Word and observances in which God has set forth his will to us. It is agreed that Christ did not hand down the Sacrament to have it applied in behalf of the dead. What mention of the dead is made in it? He orders the Supper to be celebrated that we may be mindful of his death and its benefits. Can it be that the dead are present to recollect it together? But I shall briefly add other reasons also.

The second passage is sure and cannot be shaken: "The just shall live by his faith." Therefore it is necessary for us to receive the forgiveness of sins while we live. Moreover, it is impossible for anyone to attain the remission of sins because of the work or the sacrifice of some sacrificing priest. Obscure and ambiguous causes require long disputations. This error about offering, therefore, is refuted by clear and firm arguments which in no way need a lengthy interpretation. The doctrine of the remission of sins is certain and clear. No man attains remission of sins unless he receives it by his own faith. If anyone destroys this view, he brings a reproach upon Christ. Therefore those who imagine that such an offering for the dead merits forgiveness inflict reproaches upon Christ.

Thirdly, the use of the Sacrament is profitable only to those who while using it remember the death and benefits of Christ. Therefore it is impossible for this work to be of value to the dead, who neither use it nor remember anything in it. The precedent is clear from the institution by Christ, because he orders this mystery to be celebrated for a memorial. Nothing else must be added to this institution. If anyone adds more, he wickedly defies the institution of Christ.

In the fourth place, Scripture clearly says: "Blessed are the dead who die in the Lord." In Romans 8 we read: "The body is dead because of sin, but the spirit is alive because of righteousness." This means that they are justified by the Spirit as long as they carry this body around in which the remains of sin are firmly fixed; they are afflicted in various ways so that by prayer their faith, their knowledge of God, and their spiritual newness may increase. But when the body is dead, the remains of sin are abolished. Paul distinctly adds that the spirit is alive because of righteousness. Being justified by that life of the Spirit, there is no fear nor any sense of the wrath of God, but there is "joy in the Holy Spirit," as Paul says. Therefore there are no punishments of purgatory.

Christ said to the converted thief: "Today shalt thou be with me in Paradise," that is, in a peaceful and happy life, not in punishment and fearful torments. Therefore the souls of the righteous do not depart to sufferings, but to spiritual joy and to peace. In this life the pious are occupied with terrible afflictions because God in his marvelous purpose wants the church to be subjected to the cross and to taste the afflictions of Christ. So Adam, Isaac, Jacob, Joseph, David, Isaiah, Jeremiah, John the Baptist, and other lights of the church have endured hardships, the magnitude of which no man can relate. So Peter says: "Humble yourselves under the powerful hand of God." Therefore, although such punishments are borne by the pious while they live in the body, why should it be said that there are also such afflictions after death, since these afflictions have been destined to cause them to discern the remains of sin and to repent? There is no place after death for repentance, as Paul clearly affirms in 2 Corinthians 5: "Each one will give an account of those things which he has done in the body." And the Psalms teach this: "The dead will not praise thee, O Lord." Likewise we read: "For not in death is there remembrance of thee." Therefore it cannot be asserted that after death some are still to be occupied with these sufferings in order that they may practice repentance.

So say our adversaries, that these sufferings are not inflicted in order that repentance may increase, but that there may be satisfactions. This opinion must be blasted all the more. For the doctrine of satisfactions which the authors of the Sentences invented is false and impious. And into these arguments, just as into their statement, flow very many untruths about purgatory, vows, offering for the dead, and many others. Therefore, since the existence of purgatory, as they call it, cannot be affirmed, it is plain wickedness to institute a sacrifice for the liberation of the dead, although, even if there were a purgatory, the Supper of the Lord could not be transferred for the benefit of the dead.

But why argue? The name "purgatory" sprang from specters, was then established for profit, and is now defended by pontiffs, cardinals, bishops, and canonics who are openly Epicureans and who fearlessly despise the judgment of God. What they say about punishments after death they accept just as though they were the poets' fables about Ixion, Sisyphus, Tantalus, or the like; and they laugh at the foolishness of others who affirm that God has ordained eternal punishment for the wicked.

Therefore, for the present, I am foregoing debate. In the Synod of Basle the Greeks presented a prayer on purgatory, which is extant today in the library of Phorce, in which they speak about the passage of Paul, 1 Corinthians 3, which a more recent age has distorted into the notion of a purgatory, although it is agreed that the passage speaks only of repentance: "He will be saved but as by fire." He wants error corrected by repentance. Consequently, he is speaking of the present life, in which there is a place for repentance. No doubt what is said is true, it is a simple and true prayer. But since Paul is speaking of repentance, this passage cannot be distorted into a reference to suffering after death.

On the passage in the Book of Maccabees also the answer is most clear: The truth of events is not vitiated by errors, says the lawyer. And when Demosthenes in his oration against Aristocrates censured vicious examples, he said: "Do not let yourselves tell this as it happened, but as it is right to happen." The Levitical sacrifices did not destroy sins before the face of God, and therefore no sacrifices have been instituted for the dead. It was a mistake therefore to sacrifice for the sins of the dead, just as the Jews often took up other vicious practices. For the nature of mankind in every age is bent toward superstition. Therefore, since this example wars against Scripture, it must not be quoted as a confirmation of superstitions in the church. These are the most important points which are cited for the doctrine of purgatory. Therefore I have included this argument that it may be the more apparent that Gregory's error of having confirmed an offering for the dead is clearly at war with apostolic Scriptures.

Since this is so, even the Canon of the Mass, as it is called, which says that an oblation is to be offered for the redemption of the living and the dead, must be censured. What audacity to apply the Sacrament to the dead when the institution so clearly speaks about the living and about a memorial. Gregory writes that this canon was composed by a certain scholastic, as he himself calls him. But, whoever the author was who put together this rhapsody, it cannot be denied that the Latin canon disagrees with both the Greek canons, although the Greek canons differ from each other. And they differ in significant passages.

Thus far I have spoken about Gregory. I do not wish to add authors of subsequent ages, for the doctrine afterwards degenerated all the more. And the tyranny of the pontiffs increased, although Gregory still repudiates the title of Universal Bishop and censures it strongly, as several epistles in Book 4 testify.

I could add the complaints of the ancient writers about the carnal desires and stupidity of the bishops, which, if they do nothing else, nevertheless warn us that the church must by no means be constituted according to the precedent and the ideology of the age of Gregory. But in the Apocalypse of John there are set forth terrible images which signify without doubt the periods of the church and point out that false teachers will go about straightway in the church and will oppress the truth with tyrannical domination.

The histories of the synods also show how great a madness has existed in the thinking of many bishops who by extraordinary devices have inflamed both princes and the masses to safeguard impiety, even as just now the princes and the bishops are attempting by all sorts of methods to incite the minds of kings to move to civil war.

With what tragic complaint Basil, at the conclusion of his book *The Holy Spirit*, deplores the madness and wickedness of the bishops of his age and relates that the defense of wicked dogmas is sought by means of seditions and massacres! To the Italian and French bishops he writes thus: "The dogmas of piety have been subverted and the laws of piety confused. The false ambitions of those who do not fear God are taking over the rule of the church. There is no approach to places of honor except by means of impiety, so that the more rabid any man is and the more bold he is in tearing to pieces pious and true dogmas, the more worthy of the honor of a bishop he is judged to be. The seriousness that is suitable for the life of priests has perished, and pastors with learning to feed the flock of God are lacking."

In such a manner does Basil depict the bishops of his day, to whose crimes a more recent age has added empires and tyrannies.

Therefore, since it is agreed that that age is not without its faults, it must be conceded to the church that it consult the Word of God about doctrine, just as the heavenly Father teaches us to hear his Son. David too says: "Thy Word is a lamp unto my feet."

I have not collected these examples of the errors of the ancient authors—although I have passed over many absurd statements—for the purpose of taking away any of their deserved praise. I believe that many of them were pious and excellent men, some of whom deserve even the highest praise. But not even they themselves intended their sayings to be preferred to the doctrine of Christ. Then, too, those who now put up the authority of the ancients against us greatly abuse their testimonies. Although during those times the seeds of errors were scattered abroad, nevertheless such shocking abuses had not yet entered the church. There was in the beginning some sort of mention of the saints. How much impiety has subsequently been added! Therefore the declamation of Nazianzen must not be appealed to, since his age still was ignorant of this recent idolatry.

But why do our adversaries cite the authority of the church, since they are not contending for doctrine or for religion, but for their own lusts and wealth? They do not want their tranquillity disturbed. This is the one and only reason why they desire to destroy us. For certain dogmas are clearer than the noonday sun. And yet, in order to suppress these, they exercise open cruelty and kill off priests who are pious, learned, and good men, simply because of marriage. Where have you read anything about such barbarity, that men are put to death because of honorable marriage? If they approve the ancient church, why do they in this respect not imitate the first periods of the church? Do they think that Ambrose or Augustine would have approved of such cruelty? Those men indeed would have execrated such heinousness and would have openly testified that pontiffs who are the authors of such cruelty are not members of the true church but are instruments of the devil. They would, without any hesitation, have taken up the defense of pious priests, their wives and children, and, besides, of many people who are joined together in this cause.

But after I have said what the true church is—and it is agreed that we faithfully retain and guard the doctrine of the catholic church of Christ as it has been transmitted in the prophetic and apostolic Scriptures and in the confessions—it is clear that we truly hold the same doctrine as the catholic church of Christ. I add this

also, that distinguished writers such as Ambrose, Augustine, and a
few others think the same way, if they are properly understood
and if they are forgiven for some few things which were not matters of controversy in their day.

With respect to liturgy, there is no doubt that before the time
of Gregory there were neither private, nor venal, nor funeral masses
in existence. Nor did the invocation of the saints begin to be celebrated much before the time of Gregory.

The law of perpetual celibacy is also quite recent and is defended
for no other reason than that celibacy is more useful for the protec-
tion of wealth. But those who declare that the marriage of priests is
in opposition to the divine law do real violence to the Word of
God.

With respect to repentance, the remission of sins, and justification, which we say men attain by faith for the sake of Christ and
not by works, and with respect to satisfactions, the keys, human
traditions, and civil matters, our writers have more clearly disputed
than the ancient authors in many instances. Nevertheless, it is apparent that these arguments are in accordance with the perpetual
judgments of those who have been more learned and more skilled
in spiritual matters, who, if they had read our interpretation and
method, would have approved it frankly for its piety, just as I am
told that an illustrious theologian at Paris has admitted that, with
the help of our interpretation of justification, he has begun, for the
first time, to understand the view of Augustine more correctly.

I know that many passages can be found in the ancients which
disagree with our views. And each one according to his inclination
takes what seems agreeable, just as from the same flowers bees
select honey, spiders, poison. But let deceit be removed from the
judgments of the church. I do not appeal to all the authors, but
only to the better ones, like Ambrose, Augustine, and others in so
far as they agree with them. And since these men themselves have
sometimes expressed opposing views, they will pardon us if we
should censure some things, provided we follow the clear and sure
judgment of divine Scripture. Nor let us forsake the confessions,
but let us hold fast to what they themselves had in mind and intended, but which sometimes they could not interpret. For there
is no doubt that the kind of doctrine we profess expresses the very
consensus of the catholic church of Christ, as indicated by the
confessions, the saner synods, and the more learned fathers. These
things I have submitted as answers to the more moderate ones who

oppose us with the authority of the church and of the fathers.

But there arises some new type of wise men who, since they are without God, do not want any struggles at all to be waged about religion. They praise peace and concord and execrate all who sow discords in any manner whatsoever. They think that those who contend should be destroyed as though they were defilements and pests of the human race. This is at one and the same time the philosophy of pontiffs, cardinals, kings, canonics, and very many who want to be called civil men, who especially do not want their peace to be disturbed or their dignity shaken. They hate a doctrine which might seem to be detrimental to their convenience; one has one reason, and another has a different one. All of them speak as one voice in the councils of the kings, saying that no change must be granted, the harmony of the church must be retained, as well as orderly authority.

Then they have their "speechifiers" who put forth the most vehement discourses about their view. There is no need for all of them to be named, for the writings of many are extant. But selections from all of them have recently been catalogued by Omphalius. At first, like a Solon or like the Areopagite, a certain one is holding forth about the dignity of the laws. He censures seditions and contempt for the laws, reminds people how sweet in the state is the harmony of the order and discipline which the laws effect. And, although he does not mention the name of a certain confession, nevertheless he makes it sufficiently clear who he really means. He declaims against those of us who have shaken off the tyrannical and wicked laws of pontiffs. Moreover, although I am of the opinion that this man is not saying these things for nothing; nevertheless, since the same things are being said by many very important and eloquent men, I will not dispute about what he seeks to accomplish.

This whole type of speech looks toward the hardening of the minds of the powerful so that they may not heed moderate and pious counsels but, after having been aroused, exercise unjust cruelty. But even as David once sought to bring the counsels of Ahithophel to nought, so let us pray God that the eloquence of these speechifiers may not suppress the truth and glory of Christ. And since it is written: "Out of the mouth of babes and sucklings hast thou perfected praise," we may hope that God will not fail us in our refutation of these subterfuges and in showing forth the glory of Christ.

I know that some plausible things are being said about the dignity of laws, about peace, and about general tranquillity. I am not so uninformed in letters as that, nor so far removed from the civil customs of life. I know that in the state also those burdens which can be borne without impiety must be shouldered in the interest of common tranquillity. In this respect let such sayings as these be applicable: "Evil well established is not easily moved." And this Plato said: "Just as the conduct of a crazed father must be tolerated, so is it with that of a foolish fatherland." Such things are rightly said in the proper place about civil burdens which are borne without impiety, but let not this philosophy be applied to the suppression of the glory of God. Errors of doctrine and idolatry by no means should be concealed, as Christ says: "If any man deny me, him will I confound." The First Commandment: "Thou shalt have no other gods . . ." is by far to be preferred to all things human, to the laws of mankind, to authorities, to orderly authority, to peace, to the fatherland, and to concord. Nothing is more worthy of honor than these terms, but still the name of God must be given the preference.

The prophets, the apostles, to say nothing of others, without doubt loved their fatherland and the tranquillity of their fatherland very much. Nevertheless, they were constrained to refute wicked practices and depraved opinions. To be sure, Christ confesses openly that he brings a kind of doctrine that is like fire, which will kindle great conflicts. For there must be strifes about the worship of God, because the devil burns with a terrible hatred of God and he makes every effort to destroy the Word of God, inciting ungodly men against God and dragging along with him the most flourishing kingdoms. With these enemies Christ wages war.

Wherefore, since the pious must refute and abolish irreverent worship, they cannot but be the authors of changes. So were the prophets and the apostles the authors of the greatest changes. Therefore, although political wisdom recoils from the very name of change, and the pious, who certainly are not all stupid and foolish, understand how great are the hardships and the dangers produced by changes, nevertheless, the Christian heart gives preference to the mandate of God, and with uplifted spirit accepts all hardships with the understanding that they are all controlled by Christ, to whom all things have been subjected, as the prophet declares.

This, in brief, is my response, not so much to the oration of Omphalius as to the arguments of those wise persons who in all of their counsels are speaking about the avoidance of changes and about concord. Moreover, even if godless men do deride this reply,

it is still useful for the pious to consider these arguments, so that
this kind of wisdom may not deter their spirits from piety and from
an acknowledgment of the truth.

I write these things especially to admonish our youth. The wicked,
with various allurements, wealth, and other advantages, seize the
spirits of many and then indeed hold them entangled also by such
means of persuasion as these: that changes must be avoided; that
it is fitting to favor ordinary authority and to preserve the present
form of the state. To what degree these things are to be praised,
Christians have been forewarned not to forget this precept: "Thou
shalt have no other gods . . ."

I am sorry that certain men endowed with excellent abilities
conspire with the wicked and are firebrands for inciting kings to
cruelty and to the establishment of wickedness. That is a virtue
worthy of great and outstanding men to devote their industry and
authority especially to the glory of God. This view ought to be
placed before all, that each man in his own position and as much
as he can should devote some service to the preservation of heavenly
doctrine. About those other mean little parasites who write their
sycophantic little books I shall say nothing at this time. They
belong to the class of flatterers Dionysius of Sicily used to describe
as follows: they took the spittle of the tyrant and licked it up,
saying that it was sweeter than nectar.

I return to those wise men, some of whom feign religion and,
after seeing that the foolish superstitions of previous times cannot
be excused, add to the rites and decrees more flexible interpretations in order to strengthen their wickedness advantageously by having preserved vicious rites and decrees. Of such a nature is the book
edited in Cologne under the title *The Reformation*. And I hear
that Cardinal Contarenus in Italy is in the habit of saying that the
Lutherans do injury to the Roman princes when they ascribe to
them the errors of plebeian authors, such as those of *The Lives of
the Saints, Sleep Securely*, and the like. The Roman princes have
never had such thoughts, he says, or approved such silliness. Thus
they now divert the errors from themselves. I know that everywhere there are very many who by this novel device seek the
praise of singular wisdom and who in the first place are unjust in
this respect, that although they borrow from our books many things
which have been corrected by us, and bedeck themselves with our
feathers in order to trap the unwary, they do not give us proper
fees. For they do not desist from exercising cruelty against us. Be-

sides, they do not realize that this new sophistry will be the ultimate destruction of true religion.

What will it be like if it is permissible for the more wanton characters arbitrarily to invent their explanations? There is plain idolatry in the worship of the saints and in masses for the dead. Nevertheless, explanations are being added in order to retain rites which in themselves are corrupt. Accordingly, a little later they will perhaps excuse Egyptian superstitions. May this wicked and pernicious sophistry, which is a declaration contrary to fact, be removed from the church! Any observance not instituted expressly by the Word of God is in itself corrupt, even though you may add whatever sort of explanation you may desire. So the invocation of the saints is of itself corrupt, since it has not been divinely instituted. And then, too, it is corrupt of itself for this reason: This custom itself, even though you may think the opposite, actually ascribes to the saints the honor which properly belongs to God. Let all men hear this.

I could enumerate many examples, but I desist and urge the pious to execrate this wicked sophistry. Hezekiah not only corrected the false opinions about the bronze serpent, but even destroyed the statue itself. Thus it is an act of piety to cast out the rites themselves and along with them the false opinions, which are not properly civil customs. Likewise Scripture commands idols to be destroyed. Thus let the very rites of private masses, the invoking of the saints, keeping of vows, monastic attire, monastic brotherhoods, the chain of celibacy, distinctions of foods, and similar foolish rites which have arisen from superstitions, be destroyed and abolished.

But why dispute? Those who embellish corrupt rites by this kind of sophistry do not really do it to eradicate errors from the church, but in order to defend their own authority by some sort of pretext and in order to establish wickedness artfully. For wicked opinions sprout forth again easily if rites themselves should remain. The pious must be watchful. For the devil opposes the Gospel, not only openly inciting tyrants to savagery, but also under the pretext of wisdom by cleverly preparing snares and by pouring forth pretty persuasions.

The Holy Spirit many times commands us to beware of these things. Paul says in the Epistle to Timothy that false spirits will come, and in Colossians he writes that human traditions will have the appearance of wisdom. Not only will apparent nonsense be disseminated, as many ancient and recent absurdities have been,

and as the impostures of indulgences were brought to light a little
while ago, but also astute men will artfully embellish false dogmas
and wicked rites so that with great applause they will be accepted,
loved, and held fast. Does not the wickedness of Paul of Samosata
have the appearance of wisdom? Is not the error of Pelagius plausible to profane men? Accordingly, such views as these have the
appearance of wisdom: It is profitable for peace and tranquillity to
retain customs of long standing; therefore, let the more prickly
opinions be plucked off and let the milder interpretations be added;
and let the rites themselves be held fast. This seems to be well said,
although it is a question of something far different.

These tricks have been pointed out in the life of Christ. When
they had blindfolded his eyes and the laughing magistrates had
struck him with their fists, they ordered him to prophesy by whom
he had been struck. So the rationalizers of wicked rites make a
laughingstock of Christ and his church. After they have thought up
some silly word of explanation, thinking they have now bound
Christ's eyes, they then apply their fists, that is, they strengthen
wickedness, incite kings to cruelty, and conduct their triumphal
processions, as though they have now completely destroyed the
truth. They bear off applause in their theater of operations, ac-
claimed by evil men and loved by kings, whose evil desires they
serve. But God must be implored to suppress this class of deceivers.

Nicander says that there is a species of snakes which he calls
hemorrhoids. They are small animals about a foot long, but so great
is the power of their venom that with a bite from them a bloody
sweat breaks out over the whole body; blood flows profusely from
the mouth, nostrils, ears, and bladder; bloody tears trickle out of
the eyes, and the entire body burns with unbelievable fire.

When in Egypt a beast of this species had killed the skipper of
Helen, the heroic woman ground it to pieces with her foot; wherefore, the offspring of the hemorrhoids are said to wobble, having
lost its spine. Moreover, the outcome shows that this new sophistry
of interpreting traditions is a poison no different from that of hemorrhoids. Although the ignorant are inimical to us, nevertheless they
fight with constancy and hatred, not with authority. These hemorrhoids are admired because of their opposition to doctrine, for their
sophisms and, as Paul says, for their appearance of wisdom. They
incite the minds of the powerful to suppress the truth. The princes,
set on fire by such venom, take unto themselves the flames of hatred
and become bloody and furiously cruel. But Christ will not permit

the light of the Gospel to be extinguished, as it is written: "Whatever is of God will not be abolished." Hence the church, in which
shines the true doctrine, finally will crush the spines of these
hemorrhoids. Nor will the sophistic interpretations and astute and
cruel counsels of the wicked suppress the truth.

Indeed, everywhere some who are eager for pious harmony wait
for the synods of the pontiffs and hope that they may relieve the
church or correct its evils, but they will be greatly disappointed, for
never will the pontiffs and their conspirators and satellites desist
from carrying on war against Christ. I am moved to think thus, not
only by human conjectures, which are many and weighty, but also
by the sayings of Christ and then by the examples of every age. For
Christ denies that blasphemers who, contrary to conscience, fight
the truth, defend an open frenzy for idols, and who have sprinkled
themselves with the blood of the pious, are ever restored. A madness
undoubtedly accompanies blasphemies and parricides, as the stories
of Cain, Pharaoh, Saul, and the Jewish people testify. Moreover,
God threatens blasphemers with blindness, as the Psalm says: "Let
their eyes be blinded." For that reason their punishments increase
daily and they bind princes to themselves by wicked treaties. Not
only do they go about openly with hostile designs, but they secretly
construct snares for the life of pious princes. Should we think that
these men will permit moderate and pious counsels? Several times
already we have known very many by experience who feigned mod-
eration, but who in reality did nothing except to fall upon and ensnare us and destroy our kind of doctrine completely.

I know that there are a few of the saner ones in the associations
of our enemies who deplore the obstinacy of the powerful, but their
views are hooted off as though they were scholastic opinions. Since
this is so, it is the part of a pious mind and of one who thinks about
his own salvation and the glory of Christ to seek to know what the
true church is, so that he may bind himself to it, that he may be a
part of this assembly and company of Christ, even as Christ says:
"He who is not with me is against me." Then let him know that the
church by no means consists of tyrants and persecutors of Christ
and those who either aid or approve savagery. As regards these men
let us hold fast to the most certain rule of Paul: "If anyone teaches
another gospel, let him be accursed." And when he says, "Let him
be accursed," let us not think that he has used a light or common
curse. When he uses the term "anathema" it indicates that God has
ejected from the church the enemies of true doctrine and that they

must be avoided like awful plagues, which are God's curses. Let good people know that they are defiled by association and fellowship with these people and that they will suffer severe punishment for any friendship and union with them. Of this group the Psalmist says: "He has covered him with a curse just like a garment and has entered like water into his inward parts, and as oil in his bones." The contagion of this curse is harmful to others who are joined with them and who both fight the truth and exercise savagery upon the pious. Therefore, let us not think that this command has little significance: "If anyone teaches another gospel, let him be accursed." They are not bishops or members of the church, but the enemies of Christ who are being driven on by violent passions. They do not think about the harmony and peace of the church, but about strengthening the cause of tyranny; they are not concerned over the welfare of the churches, but they are bent on civil wars, the devastation of the churches, the parricides of pious priests and pious women.

Wherefore, improvement of the churches by them must not be expected, but rather we must think how each man may separate himself from them in judgment, in spirit, and in will, and flee their frenzy for idolatry. Let us not listen to their insults against true doctrine, nor let us aid or approve their counsels or strengthen their power. "Flee idolatry," says Paul. It is not easy to abide by these precepts. Consequently, let the true church be sought; let us know that in her our prayers are answered; that in her we are members of Christ; and let us know that to the church the promises of the Gospel pertain. The promises do not apply to the enemies of the Gospel, just as they do not apply to the Jews and to the Mohammedans, as God often testifies and as our High Priest Christ says in Psalm 16: "I will not offer up their libations nor mention them with my lips." What man is there whom this dire threat does not move to flee the crowd that opposes the true church? Finally, divine Scripture in both parts is full of discourses ordering us to flee from the enemies of true doctrine and of the true church, and to embrace the true doctrine, to love, aid, and embellish the true church.

Let us not think that the church is only a Platonic state. That assembly is the true church in which the pure doctrine of the Gospel shines forth and in which the divinely instituted Sacraments are rightly administered. In such an assembly there must be some living members of the church who practice true worship of God, who

repent, call upon God in true faith, devote themselves to study, and
work for the propagation of the Gospel, declare their confession,
serve their vocation. Finally, they practice the pious duties demanded by God, and as they face dangers of every kind they practice prayer and other good works. I affirm that this is the true
church with which the pious everywhere on earth ought to be
united in thought, will, and confession. And this I hold our churches
to be, by the blessing of God, since they profess the pure evangelical doctrine. And this doctrine without doubt has the unanimous
approval of the universal church of Christ. Would that good minds
might consider of how much consequence it is not to be in the
camps of the enemies of the church, but to be citizens of the true
church, for whose sake God willed to make himself known; for
which he founded all things; which he sanctified by the blood of his
Son; and in which he revealed himself by marvelous works through
the fathers, such as Noah, Abraham, Joseph, Moses, David, Elijah,
Elisha, the apostles, and the rest of the lights of the church. Finally,
it is the church that will possess eternal life and glory and will
enjoy fellowship with God and the holy angels. How great a glory
and blessedness it is to be a member of this assembly is to be seen
in that procession which Christ leads and over which the holy
angels hover, and in which walk such princes as Adam, Noah, Abraham, Moses, Elijah, and other men endowed with extraordinary
gifts! In this procession you already have a definite place, if you do
not aid or approve the wickedness and cruelty of the enemies of the
church, but embrace the true doctrine and confess it and adorn it
with reverent character. The Psalmist says: "Pray for the peace of
Jerusalem. Blessed will they be who love her." O pleasant and sweet
thought! He urges all persons to assist the church by every kind of
official duty, to guard the purity and unanimity of doctrine, to do
good to its teachers, to commend its salvation to God in prayers
and vows, and to ward off from it all wicked teachers and tyrants.

   Moreover, I heartily wish that political figures might consider the
magnitude of these official duties which both ought and can give aid
to the church. Let them look toward posterity, to which they wish
to leave the state that has been founded. Accordingly, they ought
to be all the more anxious to hand down the true knowledge of
God, genuine religion, the pure Gospel, and churches that have
been rightly founded. Just so did Paul order Timothy to guard faithfully the thing entrusted to his care, in order that it might come
down to posterity pure and uncontaminated.

We see that pontiffs, bishops, and canonics are in no way affected by this concern, but struggle in the interest of their own wealth and not about the doctrine. Therefore, let some in the schools and some in the government of states undertake this concern. God specifically demands this sacrifice from every one, as Peter says: "We have been called to celebrate the favor of God." This particular aim of all deliberations and actions ought to be set before wise men, that they may embrace the glory of Christ. For this service God promises great rewards as expressed in this versicle: "Blessed will they be who love the church." Defense, success, and eternal salvation does he promise those who love the true church.

With this word let the pious exhort their spirits to the concern of honoring the church, and let them not only strengthen themselves against the threats of tyrants, but also fortify themselves against the sophistry of those who falsely quote the testimonies of the dogmas of antiquity and of the church in defense of wicked dogmas. It is to refute these men that I wanted in some way to instruct the studious.

NOTES

CHAPTER TWO

[1]For full details consult Koestlin: *Luthers Leben*, I, p. 238.

[2]For the contents of Luther's debate consult O. Seitz: *Der authentische Text der Leipziger Disputation 1519* (Leipzig, 1903), and WA *(Weimar Ausgabe)* 2, pp. 254-383.

[3]See O. Clemen: *Literarische Nachspiele zur Leipziger Disputation* (Leipzig, 1898); F. X. Thurnhofer: *Hier. Emser, De Disputatione Lipsicensi (Corpus Cathol.* Vol. 4) (Muenster, 1921, p. 35). On the relationship of Melanchthon to Oecolampadius consult E. Staehelin: *Oekolampads theol. Lebenswerk (Quellen und Forschungen zur Reformations Geschichte)* (Leipzig, 1939, p. 58). Therein the contents of the Epistola are also given. O. Clemen has collected and edited the different drafts of the Epistola (Wittenberg, Leipzig, Augsburg, Basel). See also *Supplementa Melanchthoniana*, IV, I, pp. 70 ff.

CHAPTER THREE

[1]Cf. Kalkoff: *Der Wormser Reichstag 1521*, 1922, p. 21.

[2]Suppl. Mel. VI, I, p. 87; cf. K. Bauer: *Die Wittenb. Universitätstheologie*, 1928, p. 116.

[3]In addition to the Wittenberg impression of Melchior Lotther and the Basel edition of Andreas Cratander of June 1520 there is also an edition of this tractate under the title *De D. Pauli theologia. Et contra perniciosas theologorum aetatis nostrae scholas Phil. Mel. declamatiuncula et quaedam alia lectu dignissima.* Hartfelder confuses the document with the *Admonitio ad Paulinae doctrinae studium* (CR 11, 34 ff.), which also appeared in the year 1520. C. Schmidt recalls a Strassburg printing which contains both of the writings to which reference has been made, entitled: *Declamatiunculae duae Ph. Mel. in Pauli doctrinam*, 1522. This writing is not in the *Corpus Reformatorum*. Only two references to it occur in CR: I, 136 ff. J. K. F. Knaake

187

has reproduced it under the title *Mel. Einleitung in die Lehre des Paulus vom J. 1520* in *Zeitgemässen Traktaten aus der Ref. Zeit,* published by C. V. Kügelgen, Leipzig, 1904.

CHAPTER SIX

[1]C.R.I., pp. 366-388; W.A. 8, 261.
[2]C.R.I., p. 397.
[3]W.A., BR, 2, 365.

CHAPTER SEVEN

[1]For a fuller discussion of the "Jus gladii" see Mueller, Karl: *Luther und Melanchthon über das jus gladii,* 1926, pp. 235 ff.

CHAPTER EIGHT

[1]1777, pp. 93-95.
[2]*Supplementa Melanch.* I, 1., p. XLVI.
[3]The Latin text is in C.R.I., pp. 703-712 and the German text is in *Supplementa Melanch.* I, 1., pp. 239-250.

CHAPTER NINE

[1]C.R.I., p. 900.
[2]C.R.I., pp. 908, 911, 919.
[3]C.R.I., p. 951.
[4]C.R.I., p. 1006.
[5]C.R.I., p. 955.

CHAPTER TEN

[1]C.R.I., p. 1002.
[2]C.R.I., p. 1006.
[3]C.R.I., p. 1040.
[4]C.R.I., p. 1067.
[5]Homer: *Iliad,* 9:312 f.

CHAPTER ELEVEN

[1]C.R., 3, pp. 679, 711.
[2]C.R., 3, p. 924.
[3]C.R. 3, p. 772.
[4]C.R. 3, p. 721.
[5]C.R. 3, p. 765.

BIBLIOGRAPHY

Bauer, Clemens: "Melanchthons Naturrechtslehre" in *Archiv für Reformationsgeschichte*, Vol. XLII, 1951, pp. 64-100.

———: "Melanchthons Wirtschaftsethik," *ibid.*, 1958, pp. 115-160.

Benz, Ernst: *Wittenberg und Byzanz*. Marburg: Elwert, Gräfe und Nuzer, 1949.

Bornkamm, Heinrich: *Philip Melanchthon. Zur 450. Wiederkehr seines Geburtstages*. Lüneberg, 1947.

Breen, Quirinius: "The Terms 'loci communes' und 'loci' in Melanchthon." *Church History*, XVI, 1947, pp. 197-209.

———: "The Subordination of Philosophy to Rhetoric in Melanchthon" in *Archiv für Reformationsgeschichte*, 1952, pp. 13-28.

Bretschneider, C. G. und Bindsell, H. E.: *Corpus Reformatorum, Philippi Melanchthonis opera, quae supersunt omnia*. Halle, 1834 ff.

Caemmerer, R. R.: "The Melanchthonian Blight" in *Corcordia Theological Monthly*, Vol. XVIII, 1947, pp. 321-338.

Clemen, O.: *Supplementa Melanchthoniana: Dogmatische Schriften Philipp Melanchthons*. Leipzig, 1910.

Cohrs, Ferdinand: *Philipp Melanchthon, Deutschlands Lehrer*. Halle: Verein für Reformationsgeschichte, 1897.

Ellinger, Georg: *Philipp Melanchthon: Ein Lebensbild*. Berlin, 1902.

Engelland, Hans: *Melanchthon: Glauben und Handeln. Forschungen zur Geschichte und Lehre des Protestantismus*. Munich, 1931.

Fischer, Ernst Friedrich: *Melanchthons Lehre von der Bekehrung*. Tübingen, 1905.

Green, Lowell C.: "Die exegetischen Vorlesungen des jungen Melanchthon und ihre Chronologie" in *Kerygma und Dogma*. Göttingen: Vandenhöck und Ruprecht. Vol. III, 1957, pp. 140-149.

Harnack, Adolf: *Philipp Melanchthon. Rede bei der Feier zum vierhundertjährigen Gedächtnis der Geburt Philipp Melanchthons*. Berlin, 1897.

Hildebrandt, Franz: *Melanchthon: alien or ally?* Cambridge: University Press, 1946.

Hill, Charles L.: *The Loci Communes of Philip Melanchthon,* with Introduction by Dean E. E. Flack. Boston: Meador Publishing Company, 1944.

Hübner, Friedrich: *Natürliche Theologie und theokratische Schwärmerei bei Melanchthon.* Gütersloh: C. Bertelsmann, 1936.

———: *Beiträge zur historischen und systematischen Theologie.* 1955.

Lentz, Harold H.: *Reformation Crossroads.* Minneapolis: Augsburg Publishing House, 1948.

Maier, H.: *Melanchthon als Philosoph.* Tübingen, 1909.

Manschreck, Clyde Leonard: *Melanchthon, the Quiet Reformer.* New York: Abingdon Press, 1958.

Mauer, Wilhelm: "Melanchthons Anteil am Streit zwischen Luther und Erasmus" in *Archiv für Reformationsgeschichte,* XLIX, 1958, pp. 89-115.

———: "Zur Komposition der Loci Melanchthons von 1521" in *Luther-Jahrbuch,* XXV, 1958, pp. 146-180.

Muelhaupt, Erwin: *Reformatoren als Erzieher: Luther, Melanchthon, Calvin.* Neukirchen Kreis Moers, 1956.

Neuser, Wilhelm Heinrich: *Der Ansatz der Theologie Philipp Melanchthons.* Neukirchen Kreis Moers: Verlag der Buchhandlung des Erziehungsvereins, 1957.

Richard, James W.: *Philip Melanchthon, the Protestant Preceptor of Germany.* New York: G. P. Putnam's Sons, 1907.

Schwarzenau, Paul: *Der Wandel im theologischen Ansatz bei Melanchthon von 1525-1535.* Gütersloh: C. Bertelsmann, 1956.

Sell, Karl: *Philipp Melanchthon und die deutsche Reformation bis 1531.* Halle: Verein für Reformationsgeschichte, 1897.

Sick, Hansjörg: *Melanchthon als Ausleger des Alten Testaments.* Tübingen: J. C. B. Mohr (Siebeck), 1959.

Stump, Joseph: *Life of Philip Melanchthon.* New York: Pilger Publishing House, 1897.

Stupperich, Robert: *Melanchthons Werke in Auswahl,* unter Mitwerkung von Hans Engelland, Gerhard Ebeling, Richard Nürnberger und Hans Volz. Gütersloh: C. Bertelsmann, 1951 ff. Vol. I, 1951; Vol. II, Part I, Engelland, 1952; Part II, 1953; Vol. VI, Stupperich, 1955. Vol. III, IV, and V not yet published.

———: "Melanchthonia Inedita I" in *Archiv für Reformationsgeschichte,* 1954, pp. 253-260; "Melanchthonia Inedita II," *ibid.,* 1957, pp. 217-224.

———: *Kirche und Synode bei Melanchthon.* Gedenkschrift für Werner Elert. Berlin, 1955, pp. 199-211.

———: "Melanchthon und die Täufer" in *Kerygma und Dogma.* Göttingen: Vandenhöck und Ruprecht, 1957, pp. 150-170.

Volz, Hans: *Luthers Schmakaldische Artikel und Melanchthons Tractatis de potestate papae.* Gotha: Leopold Klotz Verlag, 1931.

Walter, Johannes v.: *Luther und Melanchthon während des Augsburger Reichstages.* Gütersloh: C. Bertelsmann, 1931.